AI WEIWEI

KAREN SMITH
HANS ULRICH OBRIST
BERNARD FIBICHER

CHANDELIER, 2008
GLASS CRYSTAL, LIGHTS AND METAL
600 X ∅ 480 CM
INSTALLATION
 ULLENS CENTER FOR
CONTEMPORARY ART, BEIJING

CONTENTS

Hans Ulrich Obrist
in conversation with
Ai Weiwei

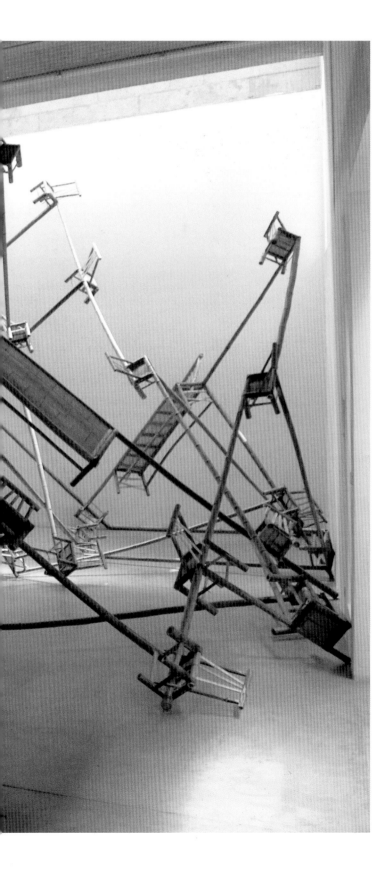

HANS ULRICH OBRIST: *Can you tell me about your childhood and how it all started – your awakening as an artist.*

AI WEIWEI: Well, I was born in 1957. My father, Ai Qing, was a poet. As I was growing up he was criticized as a writer and punished and sent away to the Gobi desert in the northwest. So I basically spent sixteen years of my childhood and my youth in the Xinjiang Province, which is a remote area of China, near the Russian border. Living conditions were extremely harsh, and education was almost non-existent. But I grew up within the Cultural Revolution, and we had to exercise and study criticism, from self-criticism to political articles by Chairman Mao and Karl Marx, Lenin and such. That was an everyday exercise and formed the constant political surroundings. After Chairman Mao died I got into film university, at the Beijing Film Academy.

OBRIST: *In this province the living conditions were harsh but I suppose because of your father, who was an extraordinary poet, you were also surrounded by his knowledge and literature. How was your relationship with him?*

AI: My father was a man who really loved art. He studied art in the 1930s in Paris. He was a very good artist. But right after he came back he was put in jail in Shanghai by the Kuomintang. So while in jail for three years he couldn't paint, of course, but he became a writer. He was heavily influenced by French poets – Apollinaire, Rimbaud, Baudelaire, you know, all this group of people – and he became a top figure in contemporary language poetry, but even then he couldn't write, it was forbidden in communist society. As a writer he was accused of being an anti-revolutionary, anti-Communist-Party and anti-people, and that was a big crime. During the Cultural Revolution he was punished with hard labour and had to clean the public toilets for a village of about 200 people. It was quite a severe punishment for what he had done. He was almost sixty and he had never done any physical work. So for five years he never really had a chance to rest, even for one day. He often joked, he said, 'You know, people never stop shitting'. If he stopped one day, the next day's work would be exactly doubled and he wouldn't be able to handle it. He physically worked hard but he really handled this job well. I often used to go and visit him at those toilets, to watch what he was doing. I was too small to help. He would make this public area very clean – extremely, precisely clean – then go to another one. So that's my childhood education.

OBRIST: *So no discussions with him about literature and art?*

AI: He would often talk about it. You know, we had to burn all his books because he could have got into trouble. We burned all those beautiful hardcover books he collected, and catalogues – beautiful museum catalogues. He only had one book left, which was a big French encyclopaedia. Every day he took notes from that book. He wrote Roman history. So he often taught us what the Romans did at the time – you know, who killed whom, all those stories – in the Gobi desert, which is so crazy. Soon he lost the vision in one of his eyes because of a lack of nutrition. But he talked about art, the Impressionists. He loved Rodin and Renoir, and he often talked about modern poetry.

OBRIST: *Did your father resume his work later on?*

AI: In the 1980s he regained his honour. He was rehabilitated and very popular again. He became head of a writer's association. And he started to write like young people do, like a younger man. He was really passionate and a very nice man.

OBRIST: *Is he still alive?*

AI: He passed away in 1996. His illness was what brought me back from the United States in 1993. He passed away when he was eighty-six.

OBRIST: *You grew up in the province. Then when you were about twenty you moved to Beijing, where you enrolled in school.*

AI: That was right after Chairman Mao died. Nixon had been to China a few years earlier, and they realized they couldn't survive this communist struggle. You know, the United States were considered as an enemy, but that's more historical. What really endangered China was Russia, the big bear right above China. Russians and Chinese never trusted each other. So I think that's why, when Chairman Mao signalled the United States, Nixon and Kissinger had this so-called 'ping pong diplomacy'. After that, in 1976 a big earthquake in Tangshan killed 300,000 people in one night. And the same year, Mao died and three top leaders died – Zhou

Enlai and another one. So China was becoming homeless, literally. The ideology collapsed, and the struggle failed and didn't know where to go. Politically it was an empty space. That's also the period when I had just graduated from high school. I spent some time in Beijing accompanying my father to treatments for his eye. I started to do some artworks, mostly because I wanted to escape the society. So I had a chance to learn some art from his friends.

OBRIST: *Who were these people?*

AI: They were a group of literary men or artists who belonged to the same category as my father – they all became what's known as the 'enemy of the state' and then had nothing to do because all of the universities did not open. Many of them are still considered socially dangerous and, like my father, politically still haven't had a chance to be rehabilitated. Basically they're professors and very knowledgeable men and literary men or artists, good artists. They had a huge influence on me.

OBRIST: *How was it at that time, in the late 1970s, with regard to Western art? What were its influences? Were there books or illustrations?*

AI: There were almost no books. The whole nation was to have no single book. I got my first book on Van Gogh, Degas and Manet and another one, Jasper Johns, from a translator. His name was Jian Sheng Yee. He married, I think, a woman from Germany, and so he had a chance to get those books, and he gave them to me. He thought, 'Ah this kid loves art.' And those books became so valuable. You know, everyone shared them in Beijing – this very little circle of artists, everybody read those few copies. It's very interesting that we all liked the post-Impressionists but we threw the Jasper Johns away because we couldn't understand it. We asked 'What is this?', and the American flag or a map.

OBRIST: *It went into the garbage?*

AI: Straight to the garbage. From the education we received at that time we had no clue as to what this was. There was no university education in the Cultural Revolution. They followed the socialist rules, in the Russian style.

OBRIST: *There was no knowledge of Marcel Duchamp or Barnett Newman?*

AI: No, absolutely nothing. The knowledge stopped at Cubism. Picasso and Matisse were the last heroes of modern history.

OBRIST: *This is fascinating: there was a limited range of knowledge and hardly any information or books, and yet between the late 1970s and the 1980s there was a dynamic avant-garde in China, of which you were a key protagonist. Somehow, in very few years it went from nothing to everything. What happened during that period? There was no information, there was still a lot of oppression and difficulty, and yet in this resistance somehow an incredible generation formed and became to China what the 1960s generation was to Europe and America, when the Western world experienced this incredible expansion of art at the time – Andy Warhol, Joseph Beuys.*

AI: I'm very glad you pointed this out. We are a generation that had a sense of the past, which is the time of the Iron Curtain and of the communist struggle. It was a tough political struggle – it was against humanism and individualism and there was, as you know, strong censorship of anything not coming from China. It was even more severe than in North Korea today. The only poetry you could recite was about Chairman Mao. Every classroom, every paper we read was about Chairman Mao, his language and his image. But we all knew what happened before that in the 1920s and 1930s. We all knew about our parents' fights for a new China, a modern China with a democracy and a science. And then suddenly they had a chance, in the late 1970s and early 1980s, to rethink that part of history. We started to realize that the lack of freedom and freedom of expression is what caused China's tragedy. So this group of young people started to write poetry and to make magazines, adopting a democratic way of thinking. We started to act really self-consciously and with a self-awareness to try to achieve this – to fight for personal freedom.

It was like spring had come. Everybody would read whatever book they had. There were no copy machines, so we would copy the whole book by hand and give it to a friend. There was a really limited amount of 'nutrition' and information, but it was passed on with such effort and such a passionate love for art and rational political thinking. That was the first genuine moment of our democracy.

OBRIST: *I always felt that it was like a new avant-garde movement, like Fluxus or Dadaism in Europe. How did people meet? Was there a bar or a school?*

AI: There was a wall. We called it 'the Democratic Wall'. People could post their writings or thoughts on the wall. We used to meet there. And there was a very small circle – China has a huge population, but there were only maybe less than a hundred people who were so active. There were about twenty or thirty magazines we were writing every night, and we had to print them and post them on the wall.

OBRIST: *Did you make these magazines yourself?*

AI: I did some. I drew a cover by hand for a poet who, at that time, was the best poet. Every cover I drew by hand. So we published books, but then in 1980 Deng Xiaoping came up and repressed the movement. He denounced the wall. He was so afraid of social change – they wanted to have some change, but they didn't want anybody to denounce the communist struggle.

OBRIST: *Did you start to make artworks at the time? What is your very earliest artwork?*

AI: I started as a painter. I made drawings, a lot of drawings. I would spend months in the train station because there were so many people there, they were like free models for me – of course at that time there was no model and no school. So I would just stay in the train station to draw all those people who were waiting there.

OBRIST: *Do you still have these drawings?*

AI: I think my mother threw away most of them. You know, being an artist was not a prestigious practise at that time. I also spent time in the zoo, making very nice drawings of the animals. That was my starting point.

UNTITLED, 1982
OIL ON CANVAS
141 X 126 CM

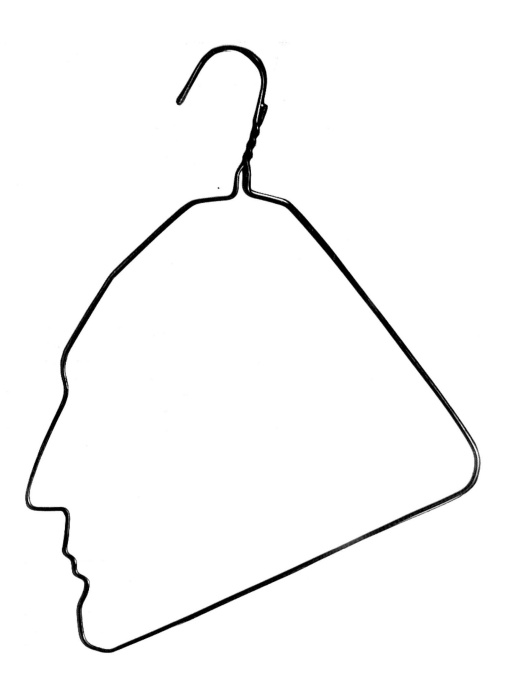

OBRIST: *What were your earliest paintings like?*

AI: They were mostly about landscapes, in the fashion of Munch – or some were even in the fashion of Cézanne. You can clearly see it. I remember at the end of the school, the teacher would give a critique to every student but he purposely left me alone.

OBRIST: *You were in your own world.*

AI: Yes, I was very clearly already on my own. I left school before I got to graduate – to go to the United States, in 1981.

OBRIST: *What prompted you to go to the United States?*

AI: In my mind I already thought New York was the capital of contemporary art. And I wanted to be on top. On the way to the airport my mom said things like

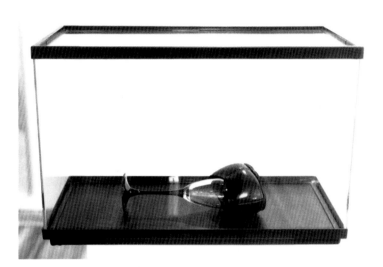

'Do you feel sad because you don't speak English?', 'You have no money' (I had thirty dollars in my hand) and 'What are you going to do there?' I said, 'I am going home'. My mother was so surprised, and so were my classmates. I said, 'Maybe ten years later, when I come back, you'll see another Picasso!' They all laughed. I was so naïve, but I had so much confidence. I left because the activists from our same group were put in jail. The accusation was that they were spies for the West, which was total nonsense. The leaders of the Democratic Movement were put in jail for thirteen years, and we knew all these people, and we all got absolutely mad and even scared – you know, 'this nation has no hope'.

OBRIST: *And so you arrived in the United States. At the time there were very different tendencies – a neo-expressionist, neo-figurative wave and at the same time Neo-Geo and appropriation art. How did you fit into this New York art world?*

AI: At the very beginning I studied English. I was so sure I would spend my whole life in New York, I told people this was the last place I would be for the rest of my time (even though I was just in my twenties). When my English was okay, I enrolled in the Parsons School of Design. My teacher was Sean Scully. He liked Jasper Johns, who had just had a show with a series of new works at Leo Castelli at the time. The first book I read was *The Philosophy of Andy Warhol: (From A to B and Back Again)*. I loved that book. The language is so simple and beautiful. So from that I started to know all. I became a fan of Johns, and then I got introduced to Duchamp's thinking, which was my introduction to modern and contemporary histories like Dada and Surrealism. I was so fascinated with that period and of course what was going on in New York. It was, as you said, the early 1980s neo-expressionism, which I practised a little bit but really didn't like. My mind is more about ideas, so I really liked Conceptualism and Fluxus. But of course at that time it wasn't popular at home. The 1980s were so much about neo-expressionism. You had to attend those galleries and also the East Village. And there was such a big mix and also a struggle. You started asking yourself what kind of artist you wanted to be. Then Jeff Koons and the others came out with such a fresh approach. I still remember Koons' first show with all those basketballs in the fish tanks. It was just next door in my neighbourhood, the East Village. And I liked that work so much, and the price was very low, 3,000 dollars or something. I was so fascinated by that.

OBRIST: *When did you start working with sculpture and installation?*

AI: I did my first sculpture in 1983, if you could call it sculpture. Later I used something like a coat hanger to make Duchamp's profile (*Hanging Man*, 1985). That time I had already done violins (*Violin*, 1985), and I had attached condoms to an army raincoat (*Safe Sex*, 1986). It was about safe sex because around that time everybody was so scared about AIDS. People had just recognized the disease and had more fear than knowledge about it. I really wanted to work with everyday objects – it was the influence of Dada and Duchamp – but I didn't do much. There are only a few objects left because every time I moved – and I moved about ten times in ten years in New York – I had to throw away all the works.

OBRIST: *The violin is interesting because it's very much related to Surrealism. Does it still exist?*

AI: Yes, that's true. It's so funny – it's a commentary about an old time under the present conditions.

OBRIST: *You were still painting at that time. There are the three portraits of Mao: Mao 1-3 (1985). When did you decide to stop painting?*

AI: Those were the last paintings I did. I did those Maos, and it was somehow like saying goodbye to the old times. I did the group over a very short period, and then I just gave up painting altogether.

OBRIST: *How about drawing? I saw a lot of drawings in your studio. Is drawing still a daily practise?*

AI: The early drawings I made were more for training myself in how to handle the world with the very simple traces of a mark. That can be enjoyable. I did the best drawings, so even my teachers at the time loved them. They'd say, 'This guy can draw so well', but there is always the danger of becoming self-indulgent. If you see drawings made by Picasso and Matisse, you see they keep drawing because they can just do it so well. I don't like that kind of feeling, so whenever I begin to feel okay then I try to refuse it and escape from it. Later on I made drawings with different methods. I take photos everyday, which, to me, is just like drawing. It's an exercise about what you see and how you record it. And to try to not use your hands but rather to use your vision and your mind.

OBRIST: *I see you always have your little digital camera with you. You photograph a lot and that's also a form of drawing, almost like a sketchbook. We could call them 'mind drawings'. When did you start taking photographs?*

AI: I started in the late 1980s in New York, when I gave up painting. There were only fifty top artists at that time, with Julian Schnabel and those people. I had to attend all those openings and those galleries, and I knew that there was no chance for me. So I started to take a lot of photos, thousands of photos, mostly in black and white. I didn't even develop them. They were all there until I went back to Beijing. I developed them ten years later. Taking photos is like breathing. It becomes part of you.

MAO 1-3, 1985
THREE PANELS, ACRYLIC
ON CANVAS
EACH 180 X 135 CM

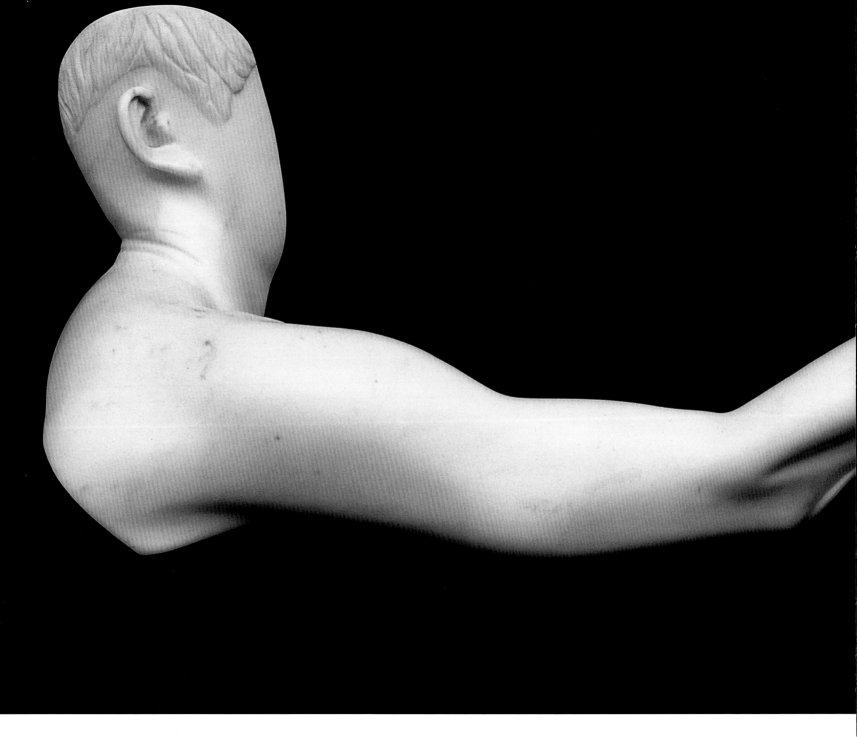

MARBLE ARM, 2006
MARBLE
21 X 67 X 30 CM

BRUCE NAUMAN
FROM HAND TO MOUTH, 1967
CAST WAX OVER CLOTH
71 X 25 X 10 CM
COLLECTION, HIRSHHORN
MUSEUM AND SCULPTURE
GARDEN, WASHINGTON D.C.

OBRIST: *That's like a blog before the blog.*

AI: Much later, about two or three years ago, they set up this blog for me – I didn't even know what to do. I realized I could put my photos on it, so I put up almost 70,000 photos, at least a hundred photos a day, so that they could be shared by thousands of people. The blog has already been visited by over 4 million people. It's such a wonderful thing, the Internet. People who don't know me can see exactly what I've been doing.

OBRIST: *So now it's basically just a continuum of hundreds of thousands of images, and it's an ever-growing archive. But do you continue to draw? I'm very interested in the link to calligraphy, this fluid calligraphy, and the kinds of geometry and fragments and the layering and composing of space. Zaha Hadid once told me that there's really a link between calligraphy and current computer drawing.*

AI: Calligraphy is the traces of a mind, or maybe an emotion or thought. Now, with a computer you have photo images, you have the radio. Calligraphy is no longer the matter of hand. I do interviews, hundreds of interviews a year. There are all kinds of sources: newspapers, magazines, television, on all matters – art, design, architecture, social political commentary and criticism. I think we have a chance today to become everything and nothing at the same time. We can become part of a reality but we can be totally lost and not know what to do.

OBRIST: *You mentioned criticism. In your early days writing was very important. You've had this link to poetry, and you're still writing a lot.*

AI: I like writing the most. If I have to value it against all human activities, writing is the most interesting form, because it relates to everybody and it's a form that everybody can understand. During the Cultural Revolution we never had a chance to write, besides writing some critical stuff, so I really like to pick up on that, and the blog gives me a chance. I did a lot of interviews with artists, just simple interviews. I asked about their past, what's on their minds, and I also wrote. So in the blog I did over 200 pieces of writing and interviews which really put me in a critical position – you have to write it down, it's black and white, it's in words, and they can see it, so you really have no place to escape. I really love it, and I think it's important for you, as a person, to exercise, to clear out what you really want to say. Maybe you're just empty, but maybe you really have to define this emptiness and to be clear.

OBRIST: *Your blog and your work make a lot of things public. Do you have any secrets? What is your best-kept secret?*

AI: I have a tendency to open up the personal secrets. I think, being human, that both life and death have a secret side but there's the temptation to reveal the truth and to see the fact that you need some courage or understanding about life or death. So even if you try to reveal or open yourself, you're still a mystery, because everybody is a mystery. We can never understand ourselves. However we act or whatever we do is misleading. So in that case, it doesn't matter.

OBRIST: *Now, we're still in New York, we are in the 1980s, and at a certain moment you decided to go back to China. Was that a planned decision or did it have to do with, as you said, your father getting ill? I spoke to I. M. Pei, who said that when he left for the United States it was a departure without return. He became an American architect and didn't go back. So what about this idea of exile – temporary exile or permanent exile?*

AI: I stayed in New York. I gave up my legal status because I knew I was going to stay there forever, so I become an illegal alien. I tried to survive by doing any kind of work that came to hand – I did gardening at the beginning, and housekeeping. At that time my English was quite bad. Then I did carpentry, I did framing work, I had a printing job, I did all sorts of work just to survive, but at the same time I knew I was an artist. It became like a symbolic thing to be 'an artist'. You're not just somebody else, but an artist. But I wasn't making so much art. After Duchamp, I realized that being an artist is more about a lifestyle and attitude than producing some product.

OBRIST: *More like an attitude?*

AI: More like an attitude, a way of looking at things. So that freed me, but at the same time it put me in a very difficult position – I knew I was an artist but didn't do so much. So the few works we see today are probably the only works I did. I was just wandering around. I didn't have much to do. And after a while it became very difficult, because I was so young. On the one hand you want to do something, to be somebody, but at the same time you realize it's almost impossible, economically and culturally. It was an excuse for me to go back to China and to take a look, because for the past twelve years I hadn't written back home and had never visited. I didn't have a good relationship with my family. There was some distance. The question was, if I had to go back, this was the moment. So in 1993 I made a decision and just packed everything and moved back.

THE ARTIST'S BLOG, 2005-ONGOING
HTTP://BLOG.SINA.COM.CN/AIWEIWEI

ORIGINAL PROPAGANDA POSTER, 1993

OBRIST: *How did you find China changed?*

AI: 1989 was the crackdown of the student movement: Tiananmen. I had no illusions about China, even though everybody told me that China had changed so much and that I should take a look. Some things had changed, some things hadn't changed. What changed was that there was more beauty in the centre. It was a little bit looser about the economy. There was little bit of free enterprise, but there was still a strong struggle, the ideology. And what hasn't changed is the Communist Party – it's still wide, still kills today. There's still censorship, there's no freedom of speech, just the same as when I left. It's crazy. It's really such a complex set of conditions. And you realize the society has so many problems and the change is so small and so insignificant and so slow. After I got back, I still felt there wasn't much to do there, so I started working on three books.

OBRIST: *That's the beginning of your famous books.*

AI: Yes. *The Black Book* (1994) is the first one, then the *White* (1995) and the *Grey* (1997).

OBRIST: *I saw them in an exhibition at the Victoria and Albert Museum in London about design in China. They're almost like cult books now.*

THE BLACK BOOK, 1994
THE WHITE BOOK, 1995
THE GREY BOOK, 1997
160 pages., 23 x 18 cm

below, from left, XU SAN, THE ARTIST, ZHANG HUAN, BING BING, CANG XIN, MA LIUMING, BEIJING, 1994

opposite,
SPREADS FROM THE BLACK BOOK, 1994

58

宋冬
《又一堂课，你願意跟我玩嗎？》
1994
中國北京

攝影：王安禾
攝影：王虎

宋 冬

此展于1994年4月6日在中央美術學院畫廊開幕後半小時，被關閉，理由有三：展覽不嚴肅；具有煽動性；具有不安全性。

張培力
《兒童樂園》
1993. 5.
法國巴黎COUSEL ROBELLEN畫廊

張培力
《防水設施》
1993. 5.
法國巴黎COUSEL ROBELLEN畫廊

張培力
《溫床》
1993. 6.
意大利·斯布萊托(SPOLLETO)

AI: There are so many artists who have been influenced by those three books, and so I tried to make a document or an archive for what was going on, and at the same time to promote a conceptual base for the art rather than just art on canvas on easels. So I forced artists to write a concept, to explain what is behind their activity. At the very beginning they were not used to it, but some knew how to do it. I also wanted to introduce Duchamp, Jeff Koons and Andy Warhol and some conceptual artists and the essential writings, to China.

OBRIST: *Was this the beginning of your curatorial endeavour? You could say these books are also curatorial projects and that you've curated ever since.*

AI: Yes, it's curatorial. So around 1997/98 we created this China Art Archives and Warehouse, the first alternative space for contemporary art in China. Before that all the works were sold in hotel lobbies, and framing shops were just for the tourists and foreign embassies. So we did it and tried to justify the space and the institution to show what was happening. And then later, by 2000, I curated another show, 'Fuck Off', in Shanghai. I think we met before that.

OBRIST: *Yeah, we met for the first time in the late 1990s.*

AI: At that time you were so young and so fresh, and I still remember the evening we were in an artist's home, I think – many people gathered to see you.

OBRIST: *I remember. That first trip was essential to me. I'd like to stay a little bit more with the* Black, White *and* Grey *books. Looking at these books today they appear like avant-garde manifestos, to some extent. We live in a time where there are fewer manifestos. Dadaism and Futurism, for example, both had manifestos in the early twentieth century, but still in the 1960s there was this whole new avant-garde idea – Benjamin Buchloh always spoke about the whole idea of the manifesto. Do you think there is still space for this kind of movement?*

AI: I think art always has a manifesto, any good art, as with the Dada movement or early Russian Constructivism or early Fluxus in the 1970s, all those things that people did. It's an announcement of the new, an announcement to be part of a

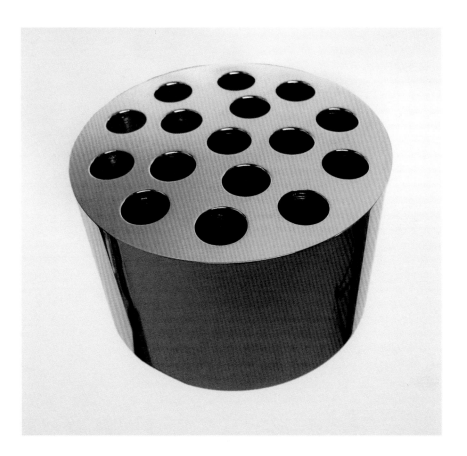

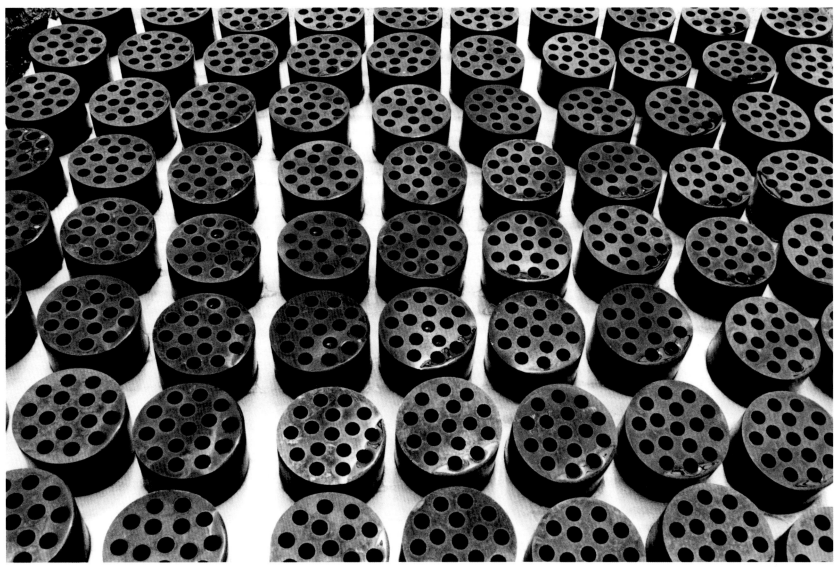

new position or a justification, or to identify the possible conditions. I think that's the most exciting part about art. Once you make a manifesto you really take some risks. You have to put yourself in a condition. You have to be singled out because it's the nature of the manifesto.

OBRIST: *In architecture, manifestos are a very different thing. You started, at a certain moment, to venture into architecture. Did it begin in America or did it start when you went back to China? When I met you in the 1990s you were already in a double practise – as both artist and architect.*

AI: I didn't start consciously. I remember two instances I had with architecture. First was discovering Frank Lloyd Wright, only because he did the Guggenheim, and that beauty we hated because … you know, no painting could be hung there. (That was then, but now I think it's very interesting. It's just like a parking lot type of thing). The second was when I bought a book by Wittgenstein, the writer-philosopher. He did this building for his sister in Vienna. I saw that book and thought, 'Oh, this guy can build a house for his sister,' so I bought that beautiful book. Those are the only two instances in New York that I had a relationship with architecture. After I came back I lived with my mother in Beijing. In 1999 I decided to have my own studio. So I walked into this village and asked the owner of the village if I could rent some land. He said, 'Yes we have land,' so I said, 'Can I build something?' He said, 'Yes, you can build.' It was illegal, but they didn't care. So I rented the land, and one afternoon I made some drawings, without even thinking about architecture. I just used pure measurement for the volume and proportions and put in a window, a door. Then six days later we had already finished it, and then I moved in. This was the time when China started to build a lot, but many of the buildings were very commercial and came from just one single kind of practice. So a lot of magazines noticed, 'Oh, we can build differently, here's this guy who builds with very limited resources, for a very low price, by himself.' It became a very widely exposed building in China. People started asking me to do work for them, some big commercial projects. So I decided, 'This is

PAUL ENGELMANN AND LUDWIG WITTGENSTEIN,
THE WITTGENSTEIN HOUSE, 1926-29
VIENNA

so simple. You just use your common knowledge and you don't have to be an architect to build,' because I think that the so-called 'common knowledge' and everyday experience are so lacking in academic studies. I had a chance, and I had nothing else to do, so I started a practice. I formed this company, FAKE Design. In China the word 'fake' is pronounced 'fuck'. We have done about fifty projects in the past seven years. All kinds of projects, from urban planning to interior design.

OBRIST: *Most of them are built, right?*

AI: Ninety per cent of them are built.

OBRIST: *You have built more in nine years as an artist than many architects in a lifetime.*

AI: Yes, it's true, we build more than most architects in their lifetime.

OBRIST: *What an achievement. But not only have you built a lot, but you have also curated the most visionary architecture projects. When we spoke last time for* Domus *you were curating an architecture village, almost like Weissenhofsiedlung from the 1920s in Stuttgart, in which modern architects build a street. Now you're working on an even bigger architecture project involving one hundred architects. Could you talk a little bit about this? Curating architecture is very different from curating art. Curating architecture is production of reality.*

AI: Yes, I love the words 'production of reality'. Architecture is important for a time because it's a physical example of who we are, of how we look at ourselves, of how we want to identify with our time, so it's evidence of mankind at the time. After the first venture into architecture, I fell very much in love with this activity. It relates so directly to politics and reality. Then I realized that it's very important for China and for the world to be introduced to each other. So many young architects are produced in the West but have no chance to build their work, and their knowledge can never be exercised. Education itself has failed because you only just theoretically talk about architecture, and this becomes another kind of architecture. I thought it would be best to have them take part in global activities, the reality. Also in another way it is important to balance the view of architecture. It's not just education through the examples of so-called masterpieces. It's also the study of real locations, real problems, and needs to include the undesirable conditions like high speed or vast developments or low-cost architecture. I think those are important factors of architecture but aren't always being consciously brought out.

OBRIST: *Low-cost architecture – that's like low-cost airlines.*

AI: Yes, or rough architecture, which is fine. It's all about human struggle and the reality of the condition rather than being a utopian thing. That's why I try to curate the architecture projects, to try and bring as many young people from

TRAVELING LIGHT, 2007
GLASS CRYSTAL, STEEL, WOOD
477 X 224 X 177 CM
INSTALLATION
MARY BOONE GALLERY, NEW YORK,
2008

all over the world as possible, because they all want to exercise their own mind
and their own problems. The problems are their own problem. Any problem is
everybody's problem, so you just have to participate. And if you have no chance
to participate, this is a pity!

OBRIST: *So that leads to your biggest project, the one with one hundred architects in
Inner Mongolia.*

AI: Yes. A developer asked me to help build this town in Inner Mongolia. They
said, 'We think you're the one that can make things happen.' I said yes. I thought
about it because I had announced that I would totally give up architecture because
I had so much work to do. But I thought, 'Okay, I can do it, but only if I'm in
the position of curating it, because I don't care if I actually build one myself. I
don't have that ego anymore, but I know many great minds, young minds, who
would love to do something and this is the chance.' So he understood me. He said,
'Whatever you say is fine.' So I asked Jacques [Herzog] and I said, 'Jacques, you
know this is a big project, but your participation is to give me the list of names.'
And Jacques understood immediately. I don't think it required much explanation.
Soon after, he provided a list of names. So we contacted those one hundred people,
and they all agreed to come. The first sixty are already there, and a group of thirty
are going next month. There will be a total of one hundred architects who, maybe
with their partners, will make two or three hundred people gathering in this
Mongolian town, in the middle of the desert. They're going to start to build there.
It will be ready in two years' time.

OBRIST: *What a miracle!*

AI: I think finally we realized this kind of miracle can happen in a short period of
time, and I do have an impact, not only for those architects who are participating
but also for the people of the world to see the possibilities. I think that's what's
good about it.

OBRIST: *This is a very special moment in your work because we started out with
China and then New York and now, fifteen years later, after leaving New York, you're
back to New York with a big exhibition, which just opened last week at Mary Boone.
It goes full circle – as a young artist you went to see exhibitions at Mary Boone, and
now you're exhibiting there too.*

AI: It's so funny. It's such an unbelievable circumstance. In the 1980s I used to go
to Mary Boone to see what was going on, and one day, years later, I was walking
in Beijing and got a phone call from Mary, and she said she would like to have
a show with me. I was so happy I immediately accepted. It's so strange the whole
feeling. In New York you think you can never ever do it, and then many years
later it becomes possible. Karen Smith curated the show, and it turned out to
be a big, well-received show, and so many people went to see it and talked a lot
about it. Mary was so very happy about the collaboration. She asked me to do a

chandelier, and I hesitated because I have done several before. But I like to work within demands or requirements, so I made a chandelier that is falling down from the ceiling and landing on the ground (*Descending Light*, 2007). We did the whole thing so quickly, I didn't even have time to really assemble it completely. We just had to send all the parts to New York, and over twenty people assembled it in the gallery. Now it looks fantastic there.

OBRIST: *So it's really the idea of light falling. It's a descendence.*

AI: Yes, it's really about that.

OBRIST: *It's also a follow-up from a great piece I saw in Liverpool,* Fountain of Light *(2007), which was about the Russian avant-garde.*

AI: I think the early Russian avant-garde had a great mind. They had such imagination and innovation about what the coming century was going to be about. Of course there was a lot of utopian thinking, and many things stayed utopian rather than becoming a reality. So when I was offered this project in Liverpool I immediately thought about Vladimir Tatlin's *Monument to the Third International*. It would come as a commentary or a pun about the beginning of the industrial age, during which England was an important factor, and the beginning of the information age and globalization. So I decided to make this light fountain floating in the water.

OBRIST: *It's also so interesting because you made it at the beginning of the twenty-first century, and when Tatlin did it it had to do with the future and with the twentieth century. Now we're in 2008, already eight years into the first decade, which is nearly over. It doesn't really have a name yet – 'zero zero'? It's a very strange moment. So how do you see the future? Are you optimistic?*

AI: When we talk about the future we become so naïve – whatever we say is not going to be happen, so whatever happens is beyond whatever we can imagine. It's just so crazy.

OBRIST: *When I was looking at your book* Works 2004-2007 *last night I became aware once more of all the different production practices present in your work. We've spoken about architecture, we've spoken about curating, and we've spoken about your sculpture and installations. There are so many fascinating aspects that have started to unfold over the last couple of years. I remember two years ago I saw* Bowl of Pearls *(2006) for the first time in your studio. We are living in the digital age, when we're accumulating more and more archive material but not necessarily memory. A lot of your works are about memory: and there is* Coca-Cola Vase *(1997) but then at the same time there is also the work with furniture, like* Table with Two Legs on the Wall *(1997), which revisits memory in an interesting way. Could we talk about memory? Eric Hobsbawm was saying to me the other day that we should protest against forgetting.*

TABLE WITH TWO LEGS ON THE WALL, 1997
TABLE, QING DYNASTY (1644–1911)
91 X 118 X 122 CM

AI: Yes, because we move so fast that a memory is something we can grab. It's the easiest thing to just attach to during fast movement. The faster we move, the more often we turn our heads back to look on the past, and this is all because we move so fast. The work in the catalogue may be just one tenth of my activities. On the one hand I take art very seriously, but the production has never been so serious, and most of it it's an ironic act. But anyhow, you need traces, you need people to be able to locate you, you have a responsibility to say what you have to say and to be wherever you should be. You're part of the misery and you can't make it more or less. You're still part of the whole fascinating condition here. I work now in a different sense, but it's really just traces. It's not important. It's not the work itself. It's a fragment that shows there was a storm passing by. Those pieces are left because they're evidence, but they really cannot construct something. It's a waste.

OBRIST: *A waste? Because you call them fragments, these are fragments, no?*

AI: It's weird, because you call something something else. For example, an old, destroyed temple: you know the old temple was beautiful and beautifully built. We could once all believe and hope in it. But once it has been destroyed, it's nothing. It becomes another artist's material to build something completely contradictory to what it was before. So it's full of ignorance and also a redefinition or reconsideration. All those Neolithic vases are from 4,000 years ago and have been dipped into a Japanese-brand industrial household paint, and they become another image entirely, with the original image hiding in thin layers (or thick layers) of this paint. People can still recognize them, and for that reason they value them, because they move from the traditional antique museum into a contemporary art environment, and they appear in auctions or as some kind of collector's item.

OBRIST: *Besides the fragments and the waste, a sort of monumental junkyard piece here plays a role. At Documenta, seeing your* Fairytale *(2007) and looking at your blog, increasingly I came to think that your blog is actually a social sculpture in a Joseph Beuys kind of sense. Do you see yourself as a social sculptor, and is there a link to Beuys?*

AI: I think you're the first one who has recognized that in the digital age virtual reality is part of reality, and it becomes more and more influential in our daily lives. Think about how many people use or are addicted to it. And of course all activities or artworks should be social. Even in the medieval age they all carried this message of a social and politically strong mind. From the Renaissance to the best of contemporary art, it's about, as you said, the manifestos and our individuality. Especially today I think it's unavoidable to be social and political. So in that sense I think Beuys made a very good example to initiate his pupils. I know very little about Beuys because I studied in the United States, but Warhol did it in his own ways: his factory, his announcements about 'popism', about portraits, about production, the interviews he did – nothing could be more social than that, I think.

FAIRYTALE, 2007
1001 QING DYNASTY WOODEN
CHAIRS (1644-1911)

OBRIST: *Now we've spoken a lot about your manifold projects, but what we haven't spoken about is my favourite question, your yet-unrealized projects. I think I've asked you before, but I think I'll have to ask you today again. What are your yet-unrealized projects?*

AI: I think it would be to disappearing. Nothing could be bigger than that. After a while everybody just wants to disappear. Otherwise, I don't know. So far, practically speaking, I will have a show in Haus der Kunst in Munich next year, so I have to prepare for that and several other shows. I don't know. I don't know what's going to come out, how it's going to be handled.

OBRIST: *Dan Graham once said that the only way to fully understand artists is to know what music they listen to. What kind of music are you listening to?*

AI: I don't listen to music at home. I have never in my life turned on music. I'm not conscious of music. I can appreciate it, I can analyse it, and I have many friends in music, but I never really turn on to music. Silence is my music.

OBRIST: *What is your favourite word?*

AI: My favourite word? It's 'act'.

OBRIST: *What turns you on?*

AI: The unfamiliar reality. The condition of uneasiness.

OBRIST: *What turns you off?*

AI: Repetition.

OBRIST: *What's the moment we are all waiting for?*

AI: The moment where we lose our consciousness.

OBRIST: *What profession other than yours would you like to attempt?*

AI: To live without thinking about professions.

OBRIST: *Hypothetically, if heaven exists, what would you like to hear God say when you arrive?*

AI: 'Oh! You're not supposed to be here.'

previous pages,
THROUGH, 2007-08
TABLES, BEAMS AND PILLARS
FROM DISMANTLED TEMPLES
OF THE QING DYNASTY
(1644-1911)
550 X 850 X 1380 CM

THE ARTIST, KASSEL,
GERMANY, 2007

'I'm not sure I'm good at art, but I find an escape in it.'
Ai Weiwei, *Artzine China*, 2003

*'They always say that time changes things, but actually
you have to change them yourself.'*
Andy Warhol, *The Philosophy of Andy Warhol:
From A to B and Back Again*, 1977

In 2006, *Flash Art* began an interview with Ai Weiwei
by asking 'Who is Ai Weiwei?'[1] The question was
relevant in that moment since Ai, whom the magazine
also described as 'the most prominent figure in Chinese
contemporary culture', then possessed a less than
prominent international profile. Within the short span
of years since the question was posed, and paralleling
the pace of life and of advance in present-day China,
Ai has become the world's most widely known and
outspoken Chinese artist. At first this renown, both
inside China and abroad, was largely due to his
involvement in the design of a landmark sports stadium
in Beijing, widely known as the 'Bird's Nest', achieved in
collaboration with revered Swiss architects Herzog
& de Meuron. More recently, Ai's name is increasingly
recognized in association with a body of monumental,
and at times unpredictable (as in the collapse of
Template, 2007) artworks, including a number of
mind-boggling interventions.

An 'architect' by accident and passion as opposed
to conscious intent, Ai initially found the process of
building to be instructive, as it allowed him to explore
the many challenging intellectual and conceptual
problems engendered by the creation of utilitarian
spaces and the essential nature of construction. But
ultimately, as a profession, it brought Ai too close to the
establishment from which he had long endeavoured
to disassociate himself. Thus, in 2007, he made it
known that he had decided to terminate his work with
architecture, preferring to focus on developing his own
personal means of expression. Architecture had become,
as Ai noted, 'too big and anonymous, so I decided to
bring the problems to the making of my art.'[2]

But if one looks back to the start of Ai's artistic career
in China in the late 1990s, when the first pieces of
significant scale were produced, he was even then
instinctively leveraging the collaborative aspects

previous pages,
BEIJING'S OLYMPIC STADIUM,
2007
COLOUR PHOTOGRAPH
100 X 142 CM

BUDDHA BRACELET, 2007
PLASTIC (LEGO BRICKS)
19 X Ø 95 CM

of conventional architectural practice within the independent realm of 'artist' activities. A fundamental tenet of his artistic agenda, Ai's love of collaboration not only encouraged the great majority of artworks he has produced to date, but is central to the mechanisms he employs to complete the expression of his impulses. Collaboration here has many connotations: Ai asserts that it encompasses the people who engage him in debate and the exchange of experiences as much as the workers and technicians who contribute to the physical realization of the artworks.

With these several points in mind, this survey aims to map out what it is that Ai does, or more significantly, what he has done to be identified not only as one of the leading Chinese artists of his day – and indeed, of modern times – but also as an important artist of the twenty-first century, period. It is a proposition that as little as ten years ago Ai would have dismissed as absurd. Yet without a doubt, although he might resist the comparison – which given the uneasy dichotomy between West and 'Other' might be construed as inappropriate, if not a little audacious – today Ai is as influential within his cultural and aesthetic sphere as Marcel Duchamp was within his. This choice of reference is important, too, since Ai credits Duchamp with revealing to him that art could be anything, even a personal act of existing, which was a delicious contradiction of the received definition of 'art' to which Ai was subject as a young man in China – a geographical context that is also significant, as will be seen. In exposing the contradictions lodged within contemporary Chinese aesthetic attitudes, as well as the powerful and dark undertones of the socio-political framework and its creative and cultural climate, Ai's artistic interventions define the prevailing moment as lucidly as a urinal in the hands of a salon jury.

In terms of the international arena, Ai's rise has been swift and can be pinpointed to the turn of the millennium, when together with the Beijing-based curator Feng Boyi he curated a controversial exhibition, provocatively titled 'Fuck Off', as an 'off-Biennial' event set against the Shanghai Biennial in 2000. Within China, Ai's career has been steadily gaining momentum since the late 1990s, though he encountered resistance from a series of temporal outrages that, in their respective moments, rocked the art world to its core, 'Fuck Off'

being but one example. For this reason, as many a great innovator before him, Ai is at times derided by critics (largely in China) in the same measure that he is lauded by admirers (until the mid-2000s, primarily in Europe). But while Western art circles were the first to applaud his work and affirm the significance of his critical stance, they continue to harbour a lingering vein of scepticism such that is associated with 'things Chinese'. The following is critic Charlie Finch's description of the monumental illumination *Descending Light*, which marked Ai's first major exposure in New York, as recently as March 2008: 'Ai Weiwei's fallen chandelier, made of red beads and gold tubing […] can be read as a cornucopia or horn of plenty. China […] collapsing under the weight of material success, or having so much fun that things are falling from the ceiling […] The piece is both heavy and witty, but after the initial jolt, you won't care very much, for Ai's chandelier also highlights what is missing from the whole China art fandango: subtlety.'[3]

Few such critics, however, can deny that, abjure him as they might, Ai is a cataclysmic force in Chinese contemporary art practice, and for reasons that are often only fully appraised in retrospect, so belligerent do his actions and artworks seem at the time of their unleashing. Subtlety definitely plays no part in these ambitions. How else to describe the methodology conceived to execute 'Fuck Off'? Or for the invasion of the small town of Kassel, Germany, in 2007 by his entourage of 1,001 – Chinese natives who contributed the human element to the massive *Fairytale* – the great majority travelling abroad for the first time and entirely unschooled in European etiquette, habits and cultural nuances? Or even the initial response to *Fairytale*, which incited furious debate and simultaneously captured the imagination of local people the length and breadth of China, prompting many thousands of hopeful participants to apply?

Fairytale involved taking 1,001 ordinary Chinese nationals to experience Documenta 12 in Kassel. This number was broken down into groups of 200, so that throughout the first two months of the event there were never less than 200 Chinese visitors in Kassel. To house the participants, Ai created a total temporary living environment that included dormitory-style sleeping quarters and a communal canteen. All visitors

WATERMELON, 2006
PORCELAIN
⌀ 38 CM

TWO JOINED SQUARE TABLES,
2005
TABLES FROM THE QING
DYNASTY (1644-1911)
136 X 168 X 92 CM

were provided with luggage, various accessories and utilitarian items to support their daily living needs during their stay. Just 'being there' was all that was required of the 1,001 individuals. Getting such a great volume of people to Germany was a logistical nightmare, not simply in terms of facilitating travel arrangements and enlisting volunteers to help mobilize the group, but specifically with regard to dealing with local Chinese authorities, to whom many new passport applications had to be made. Negotiating with the German authorities to allay concerns about the scale of the invasion and the possible repercussions should any Chinese individual decide against returning home required an equal amount of resourcefulness. *Fairytale* represents a convergence of the elements that draw Ai to art. He would be the first to admit that it is an aspect of his expression about which he is mulishly unsubtle: questioning what can be called art, who says so, and whether or not such statements should be accepted without challenge. While *Fairytale* has been discussed as a modern mobilizing of the masses directly reflecting the socio-cultural climate in China – the mass unity associated with socialism and its lingering impact on China's social structure and strata, the communists' emphasis on the group above the individual, restrictions of personal freedoms as well as the 'reconnecting' of China with the international community – for Ai the intervention was emphatically aimed at the 1,001 *individuals*. Kassel is the home of the Brothers Grimm, hence Ai's choice of title, which alludes to the unleashing of the imagination that makes fairytales so beloved by children. 'A thousand and one people sounds like a big group, but the impact of an event like [visiting] Kassel could only be experienced at an individual level,' Ai explains. 'Everyone responds differently. I wanted to give the participants an opportunity to be conscious of that: to learn something about their imagination. Would you

call this "social sculpture"? Only if it results in a force for change: personal experience is the foundation for social change.'[4]

Taking a cue from Warhol's charge that 'actually you have to change [things] yourself', this notion of art as a 'force for change' is the meridian running through Ai's practice, uniting the form it takes, the materials it deploys and the diversity of activities it embraces. This approach is inalienably tied to China's contemporary climate, which informs Ai's art more than any other single topic, philosophy or construct one might name. As a body of work, his art is emblematic of all the socio-political and economic changes that are unfolding across the country today, which are again manifest in the diverse range of his practice as well as in the ambitions that drive the work, the scale of individual projects, and the invitations to, and open-ended commissions for, specific sites that he is increasingly afforded to realize his visions. All such opportunities are potential means of furthering the process of change.

So, what of the 'nature' of these works? Ai's style cannot be discerned in an immediately recognizable motif – one might find it difficult to reconcile a piece of deconstructed furniture, such as *Two Joined Square Tables* (2005), with the shiny porcelain *Watermelon* (2006) or the sequence of black and white photographs that represent the portrait of a young soldier in Tiananmen Square (*Seven Frames*, 1994). Instead, unity lies in a core essence that is singularly undeviating: the meaning and intent of the work – the 'force for change' agenda – which alternately unfolds via qualities of disquiet, subversion, quiet rage against passivity and resignation, and sheer exuberance at the human spirit. If at times this type of an agenda does not immediately strike viewers standing in front of a work, it is probably

FRAGMENTS, 2005
TABLE, CHAIRS AND BEAMS FROM
DISMANTLED TEMPLES FROM THE
QING DYNASTY (1644–1911)
500 X 850 X 700 CM
INSTALLATION
GALERIE URS MEILE, BEIJING

because the person has succumbed to its aura and presence, or to the thrall of its rich, often imposing physicality. That said, the message Ai seeks to impart is rarely lost on his audience. His astute use of metaphoric references, humour, puns and poignant political irony has a canny habit of coercing viewers into accord with his point of view.

Even at their most crude or raw – qualities habitually wrapped in a layer of sophistication, as in works like *Fragments* (2005), *White Stone Axes* (2006) and *Table and Beam* (2002) – the textural or physical qualities of Ai's sculptures are still seductive, be they finely grained hard wood with a deep, unblemished patina; exquisitely fashioned, perfectly glazed porcelain; a dazzling mass of illuminated crystal or lustrous pearls; or even a delicately veined expanse of marble. China offers a wealth of local materials and resources that have become integral to the execution of Ai's works. Many of these – reclaimed wood components from traditional Chinese houses or temples, porcelain from the imperial kilns in Jingdezhen, freshwater pearls, bricks, tea, marble, stone, lacquer, etc. – can arguably be termed 'Chinese' materials to which Ai applies a range of traditional and culturally specific craft

techniques. Surprisingly, perhaps, the resulting artworks never invite comparisons with chinoiserie. They acknowledge certain Chinese characteristics, but refuse to be constrained by them, and would never be caught wearing their 'Chinese-ness' on their sleeve. The works are as comfortable in the international arena as those of Duchamp, Jasper Johns, Andy Warhol or Donald Judd – each of whom has inspired Ai at different moments in his career.

The innate sense of assuredness that the work exudes, either in the studio or in places of exhibition, in China as internationally, arises from a certain confidence in its making. What was read (by Charlie Finch) as a lack of subtlety in Chinese contemporary art in general is surely the tendency of its practitioners to overcompensate for the profound, pervasive sense of insecurity that dogged the contemporary art scene in its formative years from the early 1980s through to the mid-1990s. This sense of insecurity, which might be described as the desire to be different in a country that demanded conformity in the name of equality, and the overarching complexity of the Chinese individual's relationship with society, the authorities and tradition was not lost on Ai. Initially, in

THE ARTIST AT WORK ON
STILL LIFE, 1993-2000

TEMPLATE, 2007
WOODEN DOORS AND WINDOWS
FROM DESTROYED MING AND QING
DYNASTY HOUSES (1368-1911),
WOODEN BASE
720 X 1200 X 850 CM

New York, his response to his own personal experience was to deny China – his roots, his culture and the value system that had been imposed upon him. 'I used to think [the discussion of China] was not important at all. In the very beginning I remember when I had the show in New York ['Old Shoes, Safe Sex', Art Waves, New York, 1988] a journalist interviewing me about it asked, "How do you think about Chinese-ness?" I said, "How do you think about gravity?" It is there but you don't have to talk about it. I never consciously acknowledged my Chinese-ness. But recently I have been much affected by the culture of this nation, the conditions of the times and the problems people are facing. We need to look at how we respond to the world, how we use our minds, what role we can play in society.'[5]

As his career took flight, Ai increasingly imbued his work with concerns fundamental to his moment in history, but that also extend beyond it, speaking to international audiences of the conflicts between old and new, past and present, stability and progress, convention and transgression, freedom and control – not least because his interventions exist so that 'imaginations might be stimulated about what human effort is capable of'.[6]

From the first, simplicity – or economy of gesture, form and materials – was present in Ai's approach to expression, especially where readymade objects were commandeered into a series of assemblages. One thinks immediately of the playful manipulations of shoes, as in the beautifully titled *One Man Shoe* (1987), or of the violin with its neck replaced by a spade handle (*Violin*, 1985). Then there is *Zip*, an extraordinarily simple, elegant and sophisticated hand-crafted object, which dates to Ai's brief sojourn at the Parsons School of Design in New York, in 1983, but which harbours many of the qualities that would characterize Ai's art in the coming years. The minimalist-style simplicity continued with the series of sculptures centred on traditional Chinese furniture (such as *Table with Two Legs on the Wall*, 1997), which were among the earliest works produced after Ai's return to in China in 1994, but only made beginning in 1997, when he rented his first studio. In recent years, this restrained elegance is found in constructed forms made of recycled temple wood (such as *Fragments*, 2005, and *Through*, 2008), or those fabricated from reclaimed structural elements from old houses, such as the doors and window frames used to create *Template*, conceived as the centrepiece for Ai's presence at Documenta in 2007, which is arguably his most famous artwork to date.[7]

TEMPLATE, 2007
WOODEN DOORS AND WINDOWS FROM
DESTROYED MING AND QING DYNASTY HOUSES
(1368-1911), WOODEN BASE
720 X 1200 X 850 CM
422 X 1106 X 875 CM AFTER COLLAPSING
INSTALLATION
DOCUMENTA 12, KASSEL, GERMANY

Such invocations are suffused with the very particular characteristics of history, culture and socio-political ideology that converge in China today. But preserving his cultural heritage or paying homage to the past is not Ai's goal. The artworks are unapologetically intended to subvert instituted notions of culture and of the role and form of art: to question the value of all, and to unsettle the status quo, much as the interventions and actions of Duchamp and Joseph Beuys achieved. At this, Ai excels, and prior to the moment when he decided to focus on his art career, his goals were realized almost entirely through words and actions, not artworks per se. This desire to subvert the easy assumptions that often bring to reading culture, and to challenge any preconceptions and prejudices embedded therein, culminated in 2007 in the *Fairytale* Project, which is a perfect illustration of Ai's modus operandi. As he states: 'A work can be

about the experience of a physical condition, just as it can consist of a single memorable sentence.'[8] Equally, 'Fuck Off' demonstrated how efficiently this could be achieved – Ai's contribution to the exhibition was just such a memorable sentence: a neon light that spelled out the phrase 'Fuck Off', from which the exhibition took its title.

Ai's activities and actions have also proved far more controversial than his sculptures and installations. In addition to those already mentioned, one thinks of the breathless sensation of shock aroused by the triptych of photographs that show the artist dropping a Han dynasty urn so that it smashes into myriad pieces upon impact with the ground (*Dropping a Han Dynasty Urn*, 1995), or the series of photographs titled *Study of Perspective* (1995-2003) in which he literally gives

the finger to culture. His forays into architecture, his curatorial vision, his performances and his statements have provoked consternation ahead of applause, and controversy ahead of acclaim. Within every art scene in every era, it takes time for the critical dust to settle in the wake of a nonconformist, and for history to decide what future generations will think. Ai is clearly, in the words of the late British art historian and critic David Sylvester, 'radical enough in style to be relevant to the future'.[9]

Birth of a Rebel

'I was born in 1957. My father was the most important poet in China. At the time of my birth he was punished because of his writings against the Communist Party. So we were banished and I grew up in a remote desert in China known as "Little Siberia". My father worked very hard just to survive, cleaning public toilets for years, and was forbidden to write anything. We were enemies of everybody because we were enemies of society. That helped me to understand what humanity can be at its lowest point. To survive, you had to change, although not intellectually.'[10]

Herein lies the root of Ai's will to individualism, the quest for independence and freedom of expression that would take him first to the United States, and then on a personal quest for change back in China. It was necessary first to leave, for in China 'there was no private space, not physically, which meant effectively no private mental space either. Everyone was doing the same thing: or someone would do something new and then everyone did it. No one had a personal way of approaching art, or if they did by the next day a hundred people were doing the same thing. Chinese people at the end of the 1970s only wore one kind of clothes, nobody smiled. Women had only one kind of haircut. The tragedy of communist society is its complete denial of the individual and the fact that any hint of self rains criticism down upon the individual.'[11]

Ai had returned from social exile in 'Little Siberia' to 'civilization' – a tiny dwelling in the west of the capital – together with his father, Ai Qing, in 1976. It was here that his artistic training began in earnest as friends of his father took him in hand and provided a loose structure for the study of basic drawing skills. As Ai explains, 'My teacher was a kind man who regularly came to see my work. He was very old, and would walk from some distance away, which forced me to accumulate a large group of works every few days or I would feel embarrassed to see him.'[12]

'My training was unique,' Ai believes. 'The teacher allowed me only to draw with a pen. No eraser was permitted, and whatever mistake I made would be permanently on the paper. I could either leave the line or redraw it and make new lines, but [I could] not try to hide anything. I became very skilful in controlling my hand and eye, observing and interpreting what I saw.' Ai's choice of subjects was unique for the moment, too. 'I spent hours in the train station drawing people waiting for trains, and also at the zoo.' Few of the great volume of drawings he describes survive. 'My mum amazingly threw away every bit of it. My family is like me: we like to destroy things.'[13]

These formative experiences were fundamental in shaping the mindset of the artist Ai was to become, but in terms of tracking his career, the story begins in earnest in the autumn of 1978, when he entered the Beijing Film Academy Ai joined the Film Academy not following an interest in film per se, but because it was recruiting students.[14] 'I was not interested in film or even fine art. [Entering the Academy] was really just a way to escape from society, to learn something. Of course, I *appreciated* art very much, but not so much that I could get sucked into the romance of that era. For me, there was simply no other choice.'[15]

Here one sees the rebel emerging in a series of paintings produced in his second year of school – following a field trip to Jiangsu Province – and as he flirted with the Stars Painting Group,[16] which was considered the most radical of its day. The paintings do not immediately correspond with what is understood of Ai's oeuvre today. They have an unassuming, inoffensive air. The compositions are best described as harmonious; they are soft and muted in stroke and palette, well executed, and pleasing to the eye. They certainly don't appear to harbour any revolutionary intent. However hard it seems for a modern eye unfamiliar with the artistic conventions of that Chinese moment[17] to identify the breakthroughs within these paintings, Ai was already consciously looking into the void beyond the creative parameters set by the ideologically oriented authorities, which continued to align the state's artistic interests with Socialist Realism. He was already in search of whatever 'official art' was not. Look again at the paintings. They are fluid and lyrical in style, dispensing with straight lines, insisting on a sensual curvature of perspective. The accent rests upon 'moment and place', which is a theme Ai now consciously acknowledges as a primary interest. At first glance, the paintings appear to invoke the mix of oil paint and Chinese mineral colours more familiar in the work of twentieth-century master Wu Guangzhong[18] and his emotive approach to brush and ink painting than to the avant-garde ideas that would gather momentum through the early 1980s and result in the flowering of the New Art Movement in 1985, by which time Ai was long gone. They are in fact watercolour on paper. *Landscape III* (1980) shows a blood red scrape of sky grazing the top of the canvas in broad, tense strokes. This is mirrored at the bottom of the composition by an acute swathe of curving lines, which reads ambiguously as the liquid meniscus of a river or the rutted surface of a road. Ai lets it be either, placing emphasis instead upon achieving a rich, moodily distressed surface texture that anticipates the experiments he would carry out in the coming years following his relocation to New York.

Landscape II (1980) contains the familiar cow-horn-roof architecture native to the Jiangsu region: one of those few aspects of Chinese traditional culture that had not been compromised by communism, perhaps, but here equally a vehicle for commenting on the conventions

STUDY OF PERSPECTIVE:
TIANANMEN, 1995-2003
COLOUR PHOTOGRAPH
90 X 127 CM

STUDY OF PERSPECTIVE:
EIFFEL TOWER, 1995-2003
COLOUR PHOTOGRAPH
90 X 127 CM

STUDY OF PERSPECTIVE: THE
WHITE HOUSE, 1995-2003
COLOUR PHOTOGRAPH
90 X 127 CM

of the picturesque in Chinese folk art traditions that were being resurrected in the post-Mao era as a safe alternative to Socialist Realism. There remains something distinctly different about these compositions: a rebellious nature that lies in part in the tangible absence of human forms, but gains greater meaning in Ai's approach to interpreting a landscape, where subtle nuances hint at motion and energy, suggesting a certain instability creeping across the land, or blank spaces that hint at hidden depths or new arenas. When revisited in the context of their era, the qualities these paintings exude represent a radical departure from the conventions of the day.

Ai did not graduate from the Film Academy. In February 1981, as the chance presented itself, he was gone, flying to New York, before taking a bus straight to Philadelphia (as yet unaware of the presence of Duchamp's works there, in the Arensberg Collection at the Philadelphia Museum of Art) with just enough money in his pocket for the journey. A period of six months ensued in which he did every kind of job to support his studies in the English language. He then transferred to Berkeley in California to complete the prerequisite course in English in order to apply to Parsons. 'Before I even got the result, I was packed and ready to leave for New York,' Ai recalls. 'My classmate asked me what I would do if I hadn't passed the test, but I knew I wanted to be in New York whatever happened.' But Ai did pass, and he was accepted at Parsons in the autumn of 1982.

Ai was a brilliant student – 'the best student in the class', to his thinking – who on the first day of school distinguished himself as a superb draughtsman for his ability to lay out a huge sheet of paper on the floor and complete a polished line drawing of a life model before other students had 'even finished one finger'. He recalls how the other students' papers were 'covered with a grey mess that marked the path of erasers as they endeavoured to capture the form', while his drawing was a seamless flow of unfaltering lines. However, to his surprise, and contrary to the awe his drawing

skills inspired among fellow students, his professor, the painter Sean Scully, was of a different opinion: an opinion he voiced in front of the class. That Ai possessed extraordinary skill was obvious, but 'there was no struggle, no true observation and thus no heart.' Ai remembers feeling 'so ashamed' by this assessment.

Through the half year he managed to remain at the school, Ai skirted the traumatic process of having to relearn art, to put aside the values that he carried in spite of himself and the conscientious rebelling he had previously undertaken in Beijing. Like any number of Chinese students who arrived to study art in the United States in the 1980s, he discovered that an ability to draw did not qualify a person to be an artist. Fortunately, this revelation did not curtail his progress, perhaps because the roots of the Chinese academic system were as yet shallower in him than in many of his contemporaries. Ai's talents had not been spotted as a child, as was often the case with the first generation of the avant-garde, whose skills might catch the eye of a conscientious Party member on the lookout for tools to hone for propaganda use. Children displaying such skills were singled out for special training, which was considered an honour at the time. Instead, Ai had been 'brought up in absolute poverty with little in the way of schooling or possibility to enjoy calligraphy classes. My father was cleaning toilets. Privileges were not part of the package.'[19]

Conversely, the conditions of his childhood, complemented by the special freedoms that his father's friends alerted him to during the period of his 'unique training' prior to entering the Film Academy, meant that Ai's impulses had not been crushed into conformity either, neither prior to entering the Academy nor during his three-year sojourn there. Scully's words forced him to rethink his practice, but his facility as a draughtsman remained irrepressible. A fine example is a work on canvas archly titled *Dancers* (1983), comprising a series of single sweeps of the hand and brush in a deliberate bending of Matisse's famous circle of dancers to the childlike reduction of the human form that is instantly recognisable as Keith Haring's famous tag. This work perfectly demonstrates Ai's considered attempt to wield, control and redirect his talent.

Undiminished by the experience of confronting the paradoxes of his past, Ai maintained good grades at Parsons and is well-remembered for his achievements: for *Dancers*, as well as for *Zip*. It was Ai's response to art history that led to his departure from the school. Repelled by the way the subject was taught, he deliberately failed the course. As he explains, 'On one hand, you are so attracted to art, so involved, with the passion that only a young man can have, but on the other you refuse to be part of the establishment. I didn't finish school, didn't get a university degree, didn't get a job. I didn't get my green card, didn't learn to drive, didn't get married; nothing that is part of the establishment. I had no attachment to anything except the allure of art, and books.'[20]

Having removed himself from Parsons, Ai now entered a period of questioning, 'of doing nothing', as he describes it, 'but thinking the whole day through'. He began to take photographs, snapping almost randomly as he continues to do today, now largely for the purpose of his blog, and accumulating some ten thousand negatives that took an assistant two years to process following Ai's return to China. He rented his first studio on Hudson Street, which coincided with a chance meeting with the performance artist Tehching Hsieh, who hailed from Taiwan. They would become close friends, and Tehching's approach to performance art was not without influence on Ai's own attitude towards expression.

Two years later, in 1985, Ai began working on a series of large paintings that took as their focus the image of Mao. 'It was a time of struggle about painting. Mao was a conduit for exploring fundamental aspects of painting like a model that I copied more to practise painting than for reasons of wishing to criticize.' Mao functioned as the symbol of a context and situation that, for Ai, was China as he experienced it. But as time went on 'I came to realize the political overtones were too strong, so I stopped.'

Mao was replaced by the Mona Lisa (*Untitled*, 1986) which served the same abstract purpose as a life model,

allowing Ai to practise with the hand and mind in a wide range of painterly and visual experiments to achieve the texture, content and the conceptual-intellectual values he sought to understand. The icon took on the appearance of a cut-out, an object separated from its background and subjected to a series of distortions, all the while suspended in a virtual space. In the paintings, whether of Mao or the Mona Lisa, as the pictorial content is abstracted the painterly elements blossom. Even where they are cool in tone, and lack the passion one anticipates from a 'passionate young man' – here there really isn't the slightest trace of emotion, except of emotion being repressed, perhaps – they are still beautifully executed works. Ai's compositions exude the sense of an intellectual puzzle in the process of being elegantly solved in a language that is rational and contrite.

Both Mao and the Mona Lisa were chosen for reasons that recall Jasper Johns's explanation of his use of the American flag: 'Using the design of the American flag took care of a great deal for me because I didn't have to design it.'[21] Ultimately, in the case of Mao at least, it was inevitable during that time that the politics of the symbolism would overwhelm the intent and the artistry, for in New York, largely thanks to Warhol's famous portrait and the flurry of media activity surrounding Nixon's visit to China in 1972, Mao and an unerring uniformity were the only impressions the majority of the American people – general public and art world alike – held of China. That aside, objectively speaking, the paintings leave viewers largely unstirred; they possess a degree of neutrality that is an extraordinary achievement given the emotional charge attached to Mao, and to the enigmatic Mona Lisa.

Contradictions

Before Ai went to the United States, the art he produced was a specific response to the socio-political moment, whether he was denying the human form in his landscapes or bending those landscapes via an unconventional perspectival dynamic. Yet while he felt compelled to contravene even the new trends that were emerging, against the climate of the times, such action felt utterly futile. Looking back at that time, Ai explains, 'In the 1980s [in China], it was impossible for people to

UNTITLED, 1986
OIL ON CANVAS
172 X 142 CM

UNTITLED, 1986
OIL ON CANVAS
173 X 143 CM

SUITCASE FOR BACHELORS,
1987
SUITCASE, SOAP, TOOTHPASTE
TUBE, BRUSH
30 X 40 X 20 CM

opposite,
SAFE SEX, 1986
RAINCOAT,
HANGER, CONDOM
130 X 70 X 20 CM

become individual overnight. There was no vocabulary to speak of personal space, or private feelings. The whole tone of the language was socialist and collective. How could anyone articulate an individual idea?' Ultimately, these circumstances decided Ai's immediate future: to leave China because 'I didn't want to be part of this hopeless society anymore.'[22]

So hopeless did it seem that Ai never imagined he would return. But China could not be left behind. His family remained there, and a constant stream of Chinese friends – including his poet-writer younger brother Ai Dan, who would spend five months in New York with him in 1987 – and acquaintances kept him supplied with news from home and ensured that the spectre of Mao as well as the ebb and flow of the political ideology and prevailing Chinese issues were ever present in his mind. While this connection may well have influenced Ai's initial decision to use Mao as a motif in his paintings, it played an equal part in his decision to dispense with such imagery. In both choices, Ai was ahead of the trend of appropriating political symbols within art that would gather momentum within the Chinese avant-garde in the late 1980s (Mao first appeared in the work of artists in the Chinese mainland around 1988)[23] and dominate the content of works for years to come. Ai was far from China and fully aware of Warhol's work with cultural icons, but still, his personal intervention with the image of Mao – who continued to be revered or publicly

protected in China – felt like a thrilling breakthrough. 'When making this series of works, I felt I had so much to explore and learn and to express. I was so energetic that I would never sleep. I would walk at night in Tribeca where there was no one at night, and the docks on the Hudson River seemed like a wasteland. I remember being very excited about my work during those days.'[24]

Then, before anyone had a chance to cast a critical eye over the work he was developing, Ai decided that painting was 'a dead-end form of expression' and devoted his energies to creating sculptural assemblages which he constructed using objects appropriated from daily life. Even at this early stage of his career, he had a very precise sense of scale. As large as the paintings had been, the objects he now constructed were reductive, minimalist and meticulous in their conjoining. A significant common denominator was the diverse nature of their content, as well as the implied absurdity of the juxtapositions and imagery. Where one painting depicts a diagrammatic rendering of a man's body, navel to knee, and seems, in its form and focus, to exist in order to illustrate the benefits of Y-fronts, the mirthfully titled object *Safe Sex* (1986) finds a condom strategically attached to the outside rim of the pocket of a raincoat – the pocket located just about level with an average groin. *Suitcase for Bachelors* (1987) parades it practicalities externally to the world, where its contents are placed on

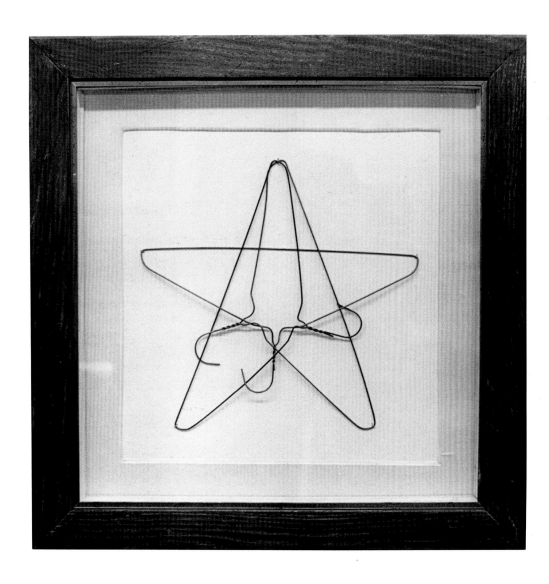

'shelves' inserted into its exterior surface, while *Tire with Salted Fish* (1987) brings together two substances rich in aroma, thoughtfully conceived to enhance the sensory experience of a visually challenged viewer.

'Painting was a struggle to find a way out. Until I discovered Duchamp, I had no idea art could be a lifestyle. That saved my life. It brought an instant end to the struggle. I understood – what I had not understood the first time I saw the collection of Duchamp's works in Philadelphia – that art could be a gesture, and that a gesture could take any form the artist chose, which might be to paint or doing something completely different.'[25]

Following this epiphany, through the late 1980s, although Ai no longer painted, he continued to test 'other methods of producing images'. In the next series of 'painterly' works, the picture plane and the object of

which it is made merge in a two-dimensional arena that appears to be a painting but that actually might not have been painted at all. To create this effect, Ai used blocks of wood, covering the broadest surface with flat skins of paint, usually black and white in some combination of layering. He would then work back through the surface – using a mechanical process to scrape or hose down the surface until the succeeding layers of paint were broken through – to expose variegated tones and texture. He further framed sections of veined marble and strips of cowhide, chosen for their illusory resemblance to the poetry of the expanse of landscape typically depicted in the tradition of Chinese ink painting. 'I wanted to create paintings that were illusions of painting – fake paintings, if you like,' Ai explains.

Between modest gesture and streamlined expression, these small works radiate elegance – exemplified in a

series of around eight works titled *Untitled* from 1986 (variously sized 141 x 126 cm or 136 x 116 cm). In spite of the volume of energy Ai claims he possessed during this period of time, he consistently imposed a codified order on his expression then, as after, as if a state of spontaneous exertion or creative chaos might come too close to invoking the violent destruction he had experienced in China, or serve as a reminder thereof. The construction of *One Man Shoe* (1987) is simply perfection. Comprised of the two front halves of two shoes, joined instep to instep, one might wonder if Ai sought out the aid of a cobbler, so beautiful and professional is the craftsmanship. The answer is that he had no need. 'It was easy for me,' Ai explains. 'I was used to doing all these things myself. When we were in Xinjiang, we were so poor. My shoes always had holes in them, which I would always be fixing myself. I am very handy in this way.'[26]

It was now in late 1987 that Ethan Cohen – son of Chinese law expert Jerome Cohen and arts writer Joan Lebold Cohen, in whose circles Ai occasionally moved – invited him to hold a solo exhibition in Cohen's new gallery Art Waves. The artist accepted and carefully selected an extraordinary group of works for the show, including a Mao triptych and a number of sculptural objects. There were three coat hangers arranged as a five-point star and a single coat hanger bent into the profile of Duchamp. A circle of raincoats were buttoned together and laid on the ground, the sleeves stiffened with rods to create another five-point star.[27] The show included *One Man Shoe* and *Safe Sex*, after which the exhibition was titled, together with a series of variations on the shoe theme, like *Cups* (1987) and *Tongue* (1987). A bottle of Lafitte was sandwiched between two Chinese cloth shoes and titled *Chateau l'1988* (1988), as well as an axe with its handle angled by a single cut and the two

pieces reversed in their joining (*Untitled*, c. 1987-88) – the 'first work where a wooden form was changed by a single cut as I would use later in my furniture pieces,' Ai later observed.

'Old Shoes, Safe Sex' opened in March 1988, and to some acclaim, if a review published in *Artspeak* is a reliable barometer of the response.[28] Ai was an unknown artist, and his style and approach clearly stood outside of the trends that were dominating the decade. Yet reviewer Sean Simon's praise was effusive, which surprised Ai. 'Previously, I only had had one occasion to show my work to a gallery director. He wanted to know why my work was going in so many different directions at once. In the 1980s, "consistency" was an important word for art – for people to remember you and for you to be recognized. But I knew my work could never be like that. [In 1988] there was nothing on show like my work in New York; it was all neo-Expressionist-style painting by the "Fortune 50" artists, like Julian Schnabel, David Salle, Keith Haring, Jeff Koons. My work was old style, but although it was a small show, it was very well put together.'[29] This is confirmed by Simon, who terms Ai's approach 'such a neo-Dadaist knockout that we in the West, where rebelling against one's elders is something of a tradition unto itself, can only applaud its audacity, as well as its artistry'. The review was thus titled 'Ai Weiwei's heart belongs to Dada'.

In recent years much has been made of the apparent tendency towards the neo-Dadaist gesture in Ai's approach. Perhaps this impulse characterizes some of the objects, but overall the work reflects a balanced melding of the Duchampian gesture with a modernist sensitivity to materials and, equally, a contemporary means of deploying both. Generally speaking, these aspects converge in Ai's deft ability to deliver arresting statements in consistently elegant blends of material,

form and gesture. Such economy of means evidenced in his 1988 exhibition has proved lasting: compare the examples of *Violin* and *Safe Sex* with the *Map of China* – or simply *Map* – series (2003-06), and *Fragments* (2005), both of which confirm these skills in the context of more recent explorations. Simon further noted that Ai was then 'a force to be reckoned with in the international avant-garde', which, in retrospect, reveals a prescient foresight.

Ai remained in New York for twelve years. Although he claims to have spent his time doing nothing, his instincts led him to explore new interests constantly, as his approach to making photographs demonstrates. Today, photography is a staple feature of his oeuvre, from *Study of Perspective* (1995-2003), from his snapshots of the Olympic Stadium in 6 March 2006 to *Dropping a Han Dynasty Urn* and the exhaustive photographic study of Beijing titled *Beijing 2003* (2003). As early as 1985, he took on the role of subject as well, photographing himself naked in front of the Twin Towers, caught for all eternity in his elemental state together with artist and poet Yang Li. This form of photographically documented intervention would be adopted by a new generation of Chinese artists in the 1990s, who would turn it into the de facto Chinese form of performance art and expression, beginning with Beijing's East Village artists (to whom domestically, at least, the origin of naked performance is attributed) and rippling out across the Chinese Diaspora, too, with the Mad for Real duo of Cai Yuan and JJ in Britain 'jumping naked on Tracy Emin's bed' at Tate in 1999.[30]

A second photograph taken some months later shows Ai standing on the Brooklyn Bridge together with an American friend. Ai's trousers are pulled down around his knees, his response, he claims, to a dislike of being photographed. 'It always makes me want to do something

completely weird,' he admits. The extreme nature of this impulse was revealed in May 2008, when, while being photographed for a feature in *Art Review* magazine, he felt suddenly compelled to bare all.[31] It does prove him largely unwavering in philosophy and response.

Ai is not averse to inspiring the same weirdness in others, too: in 1994, in a photograph titled *June 1994*, which intimates a subtle reminder of the fifth anniversary of the government reprisals against the demonstrations in 1989, he gives us his then-girlfriend, later wife Lu Qing, standing in Tiananmen Square, in the thick of crowds that pass by obliviously as she coyly, yet brazenly, lifts her skirt to reveal her bare legs and bikini underwear.

Inevitable Influences

In March 2008, when asked about the influences that could be identified as having an impact upon his

thinking and expression, Ai offered the examples of Duchamp, Warhol and Jasper Johns, which he also described as being 'inevitable for the times'.[32] This seems contrary to what is remembered of the trends that dominated the 1980s, but not to Ai's personal inclinations.

He maintained an open mind though, and through twelve years in New York, as he built up a store of personal experience, produced a significant body of work and cultivated an attitude that would subsequently drive his artistic choices and style, he never stopped looking at art. 'I saw every exhibition. Every weekend I would go to SoHo to see the shows. I really think I saw every show in the 1980s. But not of classical art. I wouldn't look at anything classical, only the very contemporary work.'[33]

A further, less direct influence on Ai's career, and one somewhat closer to home, was his father. In 1993, Ai learned that Ai Qing's health was failing, which

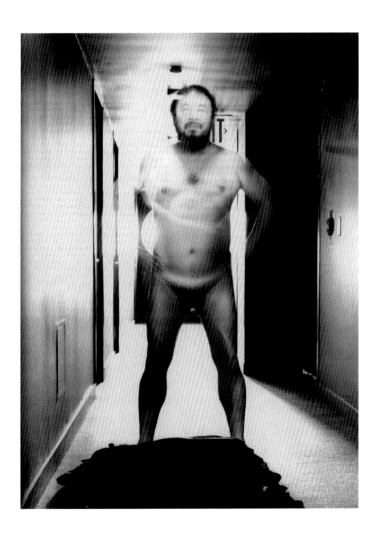

precipitated a return home. Had his father not fallen ill, Ai might well have continued to develop his career in New York. Up to that point, he had been entirely uninterested in returning to China. Unwittingly, his father was again instrumental in influencing the direction of his life. But having survived New York, Ai was now less repelled by the idea of China, part of him was even slightly curious. In retrospect, had he not returned, he might never have been afforded the experience of working with architecture, an engagement that would have an enormous impact on the evolution of his artistic practice. He also might not become quite so famous quite so fast.

Inevitable Attitude

Ai returned to Beijing in April 1993 to discover that art had gone 'underground'. Following the unrest in Beijing in 1989, to be an independent artist had acquired a specifically political taint because it upheld values that were polemically opposite to socialism and to the welfare of the social machine as a whole. Contemporary art was made in private, driven by private visions and interests, inevitably for individual gain, and it encouraged gatherings of unruly, nonconformist people, none of which was recognized as being of value or benefit to the local population. The events of 1989 had made the state fearful of letting individuals develop attitudes, opinions and ideas. In Ai's eyes, 'Totalitarian society was all about curtailing the discussion, ending debate. With no idea what was in other people's minds, eventually people lost sight of what was in their own minds. This meant they could have no idea of the reality in which they or other people were living.'

Instead of resigning himself to the situation, Ai actively responded to it. Having spent his 'best years in New York doing nothing' – while experiencing possibly the most intellectually profitable period of his life to that point – Ai again sat back to observe, unconcerned about what would be his next move. It came soon: his first act, in mid-1994, was to challenge the monopoly of figurative painting by publishing a series of books – the *Black* (1994), *White* (1995) and *Grey* (1997) books – that collated plans, installation concepts, performance ideas and generally unrealizable artistic notions which he made public for the first time. He describes his choice of media thus: 'A book could contain things that could not otherwise be placed in the public realm. Also, it allowed the artists to show works that could not practically be realized. It was all about exploring the imagination.' The books were the perfect tool for communicating previously marginal and invisible positions, and they were simultaneously a marvellous vehicle for alerting the art world to Ai's personal worldview.

As the content of the books evidences, through the 1990s the public arena in China was incrementally opening up to artists, such that in 2000 Ai himself could make a very loud public statement about the state of Chinese art and culture in the form of the off-Biennial exhibition in Shanghai titled 'Fuck Off', which included works from some forty-six aggressively experimental, established and emerging artists. The show was like a performance itself. Ai describes it as 'a very pure statement about Chinese art'.[34] 'Fuck Off' demonstrated Ai's premise that 'Artists are not in a position to decide the conditions imposed upon them but they can make statements about those conditions.'[35]

Typically in China, in order for such sentiments to resonate, the authorities had to feel goaded into closing the exhibition down. One might suggest, then, that similar to the way in which Duchamp's *Fountain* – the urinal – *needed* to be rejected by the system responsible

for 'those conditions', Ai needed 'Fuck Off' to be shut down in order to reinforce the urgency of challenging, and changing, the Chinese system. It nearly didn't happen, simply because the local authorities in Shanghai wavered indecisively about what to do. This allowed enough people to see the works, which, given that the show's timing coincided with the Shanghai Biennial, was quite a crowd. And in spite of the chaotic nature of the exhibition and the uneven quality of the exhibits, to proclaim this the 'best show in a decade' was P.S.1 director Alanna Heiss, who was one of those there for the Biennial. As the initial wave of visitors disappeared from view, the authorities finally ordered the exhibition closed, thereby ensuring that the myth would live on long after the actual exhibition and all its contents had blurred into one exhilarating, sensational moment in Chinese contemporary art history.

Shortly afterward Ai was afforded the opportunity to make a very public personal statement in Beijing, with the unveiling of *Concrete* (2000), a work commissioned for a public space – both the first of their kind in the capital. *Concrete* was conceived to serve as a water-feature and public seating area on the grounds of the chichi residential-commercial complex Soho New Town, whose name embodied its aspirations. Adopting an exaggerated monumental scale, *Concrete* stands as a tongue-in-cheek homage to the socialist-industrial aspirations of China, old and new. Mao once said he hoped to see a sea of chimneys radiating out from Tiananmen Square. The new generation, typified by the property developers, preferred to invoke New York's SoHo district as their vision of what modern China should look like. Mirroring the form of a monstrous chimney stack rising from a heavy, slab-like concrete base, *Concrete* quietly echoed the skyline of the massive energy plant that sat directly north of this 'modern' site, at odds with the contemporary vision of Soho New Town. But *Concrete*'s darkest seam of humour lay in its reminder to the developers that having a modern mind-set or outlook means little when one is embroiled in the immutable and complex political imbroglio of Chinese bureaucracy, which promotes material growth at the expense of real personal freedoms. 'As a public sculpture, *Concrete* was intended to show how to retain the raw

and bold qualities of an architectural element within an upper-class neighbourhood,' Ai explains. 'Today China is so trendy: everybody follows the trend towards making everything luxurious and decorated with "design". *Concrete* aimed to contradict that thinking: to make a statement against that type of meaningless lifestyle.'[36]

Practical Choices

'In 1997, I started making furniture. By then I already had a profound knowledge of Chinese artefacts, jade, silk, bronze, wood. I was deeply impressed with the objects that had been made in the past five thousand years, and how these reflected the thinking of the people who ordered them, who designed them and who created them: what it was that they wanted to express through these objects, as well as the technical difficulties they had to overcome. I came back from New York and jumped into another world. I wanted to see how to work with it, to overcome it. The furniture began there; combining the New York experience with the Chinese conditions, its history and my understanding of all.'[37]

Ai has always been practical about the choice of materials he brings to the work. Practicality does not, of course, refer to the works themselves – the furniture series, for instance, is not intended to function outside of the realm of artistic expression – but to the means by which the materials can be married with available skills in order to produce a work. If this sounds contradictory, that's because it is. Delightfully so, to Ai's way of thinking: a 'practical means of carrying out useless projects'.

'Useless' is a word Ai employed when first describing to me his state of existence in New York after he acquitted himself of his studies at Parsons. He followed a similarly 'aimless' routine back in Beijing where, 'returning from the USA with no money', he moved back in with his mother, 'playing cards all day with my brother, doing absolutely nothing, for years' until, in 1999, he built his own Studio House because 'my mother was growing tired of me'. The need to find his own place, and the bold decision to build it himself, was the springboard

BENCH, 2004
IRONWOOD FROM DISMANTLED
TEMPLES OF THE QING
DYNASTY (1644-1911)
400 X Ø 55 CM
INSTALLATION
KUNSTHALLE BERN

following pages,
OIL SPILLS, 2006
PORCELAIN
12 PIECES, EACH BETWEEN
Ø 13 AND 119 CM
INSTALLATION
GALERIE URS MEILE, BEIJING

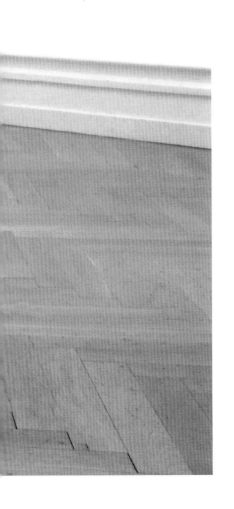

that launched Ai into architecture, which would occupy much of his energy and creative output during the next several years. He had not been entirely idle. In addition to the three books he produced with the help of various artists and editors, he had also established in 1998 the China Art Archives and Warehouse (CAAW), together with some like-minded partners,[38] as a private, non-commercial exhibition space for experimental art. It continues to hold rank among more cutting-edge artists and against the swelling tide of galleries in the capital as a place to see provocative, impulsive art.

The claim to a 'useless' life is, then, a stance, but one that is relevant to the work Ai creates, in terms of the content, the form and the impetus behind it, but also in terms of what it means to him to rebel. Did he inherit this from his father? Ai Qing ought to have been a most useful asset in building a new China, yet, once denounced, all his learning and intellect was rendered useless. In the aftermath of the events of 1989 and the mood of deflation that ensued, the avant-garde largely followed the view that 'If you're no use at all, who'll come to bother you?' Conversely, Ai repeatedly invites people to 'bother' him, while actively attempting to bother society with the 'experience' of contemporary art in a multitude of ways.

The philosopher Zhuangzi is quoted as saying 'All men know the use of usefulness, but none know the use of uselessness'.[39] Ai apparently does. Uselessness has a creative aspect that feeds the methods he deploys in making art, especially the challenges he gives his assistants to experiment with form, materials and traditions. But although Ai places great, often-awkward demands on his assistants, the anticipated resolutions lie within the familiar aspects of the local traditions. The assistants are an essential element in the problem-solving process involved in realizing Ai's works, which would be impossible alone. 'We have a very long and specific history in China,' Ai contends. 'This society never believed in science, it never believed in democracy. We believe in emotions, in this strange feeling of nature – our culture is based on that.' This interest in the politics of cultural heritage led Ai to draw on traditional

skills that had been rendered useless to modern society and turn them into practical ways of addressing and embracing modern-day local conditions.

'It interests me to try and create something with no purpose to it; but to make art also creates a purpose,' he says. In so far as the 'useless' objects Ai creates are intended to serve the greatest purpose of prompting questions about the value of culture and of art, they are all conceived with a function in mind. The function begins with the process of convincing the assistants to execute a concept. These are highly skilled craftsmen liable to feel insulted by requests to direct their skills at such absurd tasks as freezing a flow of urine in fine porcelain, reconfiguring fine examples of classical furniture into dysfunctional forms or creating perfect, lusciously glazed replicas of watermelons. This tension goes to the heart of the 'culture' problem: who decides what is precious, of enduring value to society, and for what reasons? Ai firmly believes that 'All humanity lives according to certain immutable conditions of life, and of society. That has always been so. Artists should always aim to challenge these whenever the opportunity arises.'[40]

Taking his own advice, Ai has used a great number of 'useless' objects to challenge these conditions. There are benches that cannot be sat upon, tables that refuse to carry objects, a bed that can't be laid on, cupboards in which things cannot be stored, a solid marble basket therefore unable to 'hold' objects, or even to be held due to its weight, and delicate girls' dresses fashioned from porcelain into rigid suggestions of actual garments. What is extraordinary in every one of these works is the degree of flawless craftsmanship that was brought to its creation. The workmanship in a single drop of oil (the porcelain *Oil Spills*, 2006), or in the replication of an ordinary lump of coal (*Mei Le*, 2007), or in the carving of a simple door from a piece of hard and unyielding marble (forty such pieces brought together for *Monumental Junkyard*, 2006) is staggering. Each of these feats took months, if not years – in the case of *Mei Le*, for example – to realize. *Mei Le* is a sculptural installation formed of cast fibreglass coated with Chinese

MEILE, 2007
LACQUER ON FIBREGLASS
167 PIECES
Ø 700 CM, HEIGHT VARIES FROM
8 TO 28 CM

MEILE, 2007
LACQUER ON FIBREGLASS
167 PIECES
Ø 700 CM, HEIGHT VARIES FROM
8 TO 28 CM

TABLE WITH TWO LEGS, 2005
TABLE FROM THE LATE MING
OR EARLY QING DYNASTY
(1368-1911)
70 X 186 X 115 CM

CORNER TABLE, 2006
TABLE FROM THE LATE MING
OR EARLY QING DYNASTY
(1368-1911)
116 X 116 X 116 CM

lacquer, which requires approximately fifteen coats to achieve an exemplary glossy liquid sheen. That done, the individual pieces were then abandoned to the elements in the courtyard of Ai's studio/house, in order to obtain a suitably weathered texture appropriate to coal.

Ai has an intuitive sense of compatibility when selecting materials. He is equally adept at determining how other components – such as bricks made of compressed tea or the pieces of reclaimed wood that he amasses from far and wide, cleans up, and then amalgamates in works like the *Map of China* series – can be reconfigured as individual building blocks of a work. 'I always have the materials first',,he asserts. 'Sometimes they sit in the studio for years before I decide how to use them. I have always been fascinated by materials. I collect things without knowing what I will do with them, and then suddenly there's enlightenment. I have to learn to be at ease with them. Before that they sit uncomfortably in the studio, out of context, unfamiliar. But one day I suddenly see them differently. That's when I make a drawing, and the work begins.'[41]

In a slightly different vein, this approach of commandeering skill, time and mental and physical

energy to explore useless pursuits is further evident in a series of four video projects that Ai produced between 2003 and 2005. Their mundane titles give a clue to the focus of their content: *Beijing 2003* (2003),[42] *Chang'an Boulevard* (2004), *Beijing: The Second Ring* (2005) and *Beijing: The Third Ring* (2005). The videos examine various traffic circulation patterns in the capital, as well as encompassing many mundane scenes of daily life in the city. The style and approach is straight out of Warhol's *Empire State*, a film made in 1964, which consists of a one-shot frame of the Empire State Building with a screening time of eight hours. *Beijing 2003* far outlasts *Empire State*, comprising 1,500 hours of footage, but even this pales before the 150 hours of footage Ai amassed in the filmed documentation of *Fairytale*. *Beijing: The Second Ring* and *Beijing: The Third Ring* are of a slightly shorter length: under two hours each. They show traffic moving around the capital's second and third ring roads, shot from the bridges that straddle these concentric highways at regular intervals. For variety, Ai invokes two opposing weather situations: one sunny, the other overcast. These at least imply a degree of action, if only a mind-numbingly monotonous yet mesmerizing motion. 'I want to throw art into a different condition, or dimension, so I tend to have

previous pages,
BED, 2004
IRONWOOD FROM DISMANTLED
TEMPLES OF THE QING
DYNASTY (1644-1911)
200 X 600 CM

below,
STOOL, 1997
STOOLS FROM THE QING
DYNASTY (1644-1911)
59 X 60 X 28 CM

different works going on at the same time. This means I have a different sense of time as things unfold,' Ai says.

In 2003, in tandem with the video work *Beijing 2003*, Ai created *Beijing 10/2003*, using a camera to produce a photographic record of a journey through the city: one frame snapped every five minutes resulting in the 1,719 images that appear in the book. *Beijing 10/2003* is not the most compelling of visual sequences. There is little context in which to read, decipher or interpret the individual images, the random nature of which makes them singly unresolved. But like Warhol's film, this type of work is not meant to be gripping. It is about life as lived and experienced today. Similar to Ai's video works, there is no action – neither crash, nor road rage, nor dramatic car chase – but there is that kind of beauty apparent when we're detached from the gridlock, not stuck in it inhaling the bad fumes and bad vibes of sheer frustration. Then, the silent stop-start flow softens into abstract ribbons of colour that make commuting almost romantic. 'I think what happens around us is often more massive than what we can interpret,' Ai explains. 'I am Chinese. I live in Beijing. My state of mind is necessarily affected by the environment. I look at what is familiar to me to interpret this. It is not about nostalgia for the

city. Artists are always seeking a resource or approach that can make the work relevant [to the audience], or show the understanding or interpretation of [a situation or condition]. This is my sense of the massive change that has happened in this city, which we are all part of. I wanted to find an almost mathematical and unemotional way to show this: to show the powerlessness of the people, and the blind nature of the redevelopment.'[43]

Form

The greater portion of redevelopment in Beijing has been architectural. While only a small fraction of Ai's architectural projects can be found in the capital, they have exerted a significant influence on the style of the buildings erected to create the new art zones appearing on the city perimeters. This experience of working with architecture and of realizing a large number of building projects has also functioned as a visible force in the art Ai produced from the early 2000s onwards. One of the arresting aspects of his large-scale installation works, such as the 'baroque' *Fragments* (2005), the Kassel centrepiece *Template* (2007), and *Through* (2007-8), or

even *In Between* (2000) and *Forever* (2003) is the way in which individual components come together to achieve a cogent physical structure and enjoy a symbiotic relationship with space. *Fragments'* exalted arches suggest the ambitious reach of medieval barrelled vaults as the succession of wooden beams rise heavenward together in what from the ground appears to be a rustic circle of shamanistic significance. Only when the installation is viewed from above can one discern the map of China that is marked out by the span of its limbs and the objects incorporated into it.

Through further develops Ai's fascination with structural dynamics. It is an extraordinary piece. 'You have to see it to understand,' the artist states. 'It took almost a year to create, with ten carpenters, and using no nails.' *Through* is a perfect example of how a sense of monumentality pervades Ai's large-scale installations. Covering 200 square metres, it centres on a simple juxtaposition of reclaimed columns from defunct temples and examples of Ming tables. Viewers can walk around and 'through' it. Monumental in his studio in Beijing, and stifling (or stifled) at its debut in Sydney in 2008, the cage-like structure had itself become caged in. *Through* is suffused with a penetrating sense of menace rarely so overtly present in Ai's work. His inspiration: 'I had been thinking about the feeling of unease people have facing huge structures.' Certainly *Through* suggests a powerful bully imposing its will on the powerless (the tables, which are made to look so small by the massive beams that impale them to the ground). It is a metaphor for human experience, where frailty is pitted against might, and yet refuses to yield entirely: like David before Goliath, or, given the context of China and the possible interpretation of the beams as the reigning force of communism in the act of subjugating the simple, honest masses of the people, represented by the humble tables.

THROUGH, 2007-08
TABLES, BEAMS AND
PILLARS FROM DIS-
MANTLED TEMPLES
OF THE QING DYNASTY
(1644-1911)
550 X 850 X 1380 CM
INSTALLATION
SHERMAN
CONTEMPORARY ART
FOUNDATION, SYDNEY

CUBIC METER TABLES, 2006
HUANGHUALI WOOD
13 PIECES, EACH 100 X 100 X
100 CM
INSTALLATION
GALLERIA CONTINUA, BEIJING

Ai's work with spatial form has its roots in his furniture, albeit on a smaller scale. *Cubic Meter Tables* (2006) create a Judd-like series of framed spaces, which are explored again more recently in a series of pairs of huge wooden chests (*Moon Chest*) produced in 2008. Here, form is consistently geometric in terms of each of the several elements of which it consists: circles, ellipses, rectangles and squares, and by extrapolation, positive and negative cubes and spheres. Each one has been perfectly calculated to determine the mathematical relationship between individual components, with a further sense of scale similar to that which is evident in the arrangement of concentric rings in *Descending Light*. Each of these works exudes a sense of order and stillness but also invites light to playfully alter the shapes and sense of the pieces, and the spaces they create, at different times of day and in various environs.

As evidenced by his light installations, Ai's exploration of form in space is not restricted to wood. A further example is the porcelain *Pillars* (2006), glazed with typical local mineral colours to represent mammoth versions of vessels that can be traced back to various Chinese dynastic styles, where they usually existed on a far more modest scale. Scale lends their presence

authority and solidity, just as their existence inspires awe over how hard it was to create them. A kiln had to be built for each one, the gestation period of the firing was as fraught as that of any foetus, and the result was equally unpredictable and uncertain, until that final moment of release from the womb of its chamber. Many pillars did not survive their baptism of fire, which only lends authority to those that did, a sensation felt in their stoic rigidity and soft patina.

The visual perfection of all these forms leaves a lingering impression. There's never any clutter; nothing is overdone. At times, the air of perfection is almost too much. But there has always been an edge of humour in Ai's work that is never quite permitted to descend into cynicism, a wry undertone that is its saving grace.

Destruction

To clear a path for the new, one has to destroy, clear away the old. As destruction is implicit in the photographic work *Study of Perspective*, many of Ai's other works exude a destructive undertone. The pieces of furniture are utterly confounded by the alteration of line, form

below,
COLORED VASES, 2006
51 NEOLITHIC VASES (5000-3000 BC),
INDUSTRIAL PAINT
HEIGHT VARIES FROM 20 TO 40 CM

previous pages,
PILLARS, 2006
16 PORCELAIN PILLARS HEIGHT VARIES
FROM 178 TO 219 CM
INSTALLATION
KUNSTHAUS GRAZ

and planar juxtaposition of their proportion and order. The actions imposed on antique Neolithic and Han pots represent the destruction of conventional or established values. The fact that the examples Ai destroys are *actual* antiquities is essential, for although postmodern rules might allow for substitution to give credence to a concept, the impact of using a replica would not yield the same sensation.[44] From those few early acts, the process has been expanded in great measure: a succession of pots have been doused in brightly coloured household paint, or defaced with well-known brand names. On several occasions, the artist spontaneously smashed a pot in his studio to the extraordinary thrill of visitors present who couldn't quite believe their eyes but were very pleased to have witnessed it. More recently, a multitude of pots have been obliterated entirely by being ground to dust. Between 2007 and

mid-2008, Ai conceived *Untitled*, which incorporates thirty-five glass specimen jars, each filled with several kilos of extraordinarily fine dust created by grinding down dozens of pots. Similarly, a series of porcelain works created in 1996-97 'after' exemplary pieces from the reigns of Emperors Kangxi and Qianlong was predicated on a conscious deception of authentic antiques (valuable) with modern replicas (worth less, and considered decorative, rather than pure, art). These transpositions again undermine individual and social values, disrupting the logic brought to formalizing those values and the way in which we appraise high art versus mediocrity, a simulacrum versus the real thing.

Ai's work with light, in the form of a series of chandeliers that began with the monumental hanging piece simply titled *Chandelier* in 2002 and culminated in *Descending*

Light in 2008, arguably comes under the same heading.[45] Each of the four stages within this progression of works – which includes the opulent *Boomerang* (2006) created in Australia and *Fountain of Light* (2007) presented at Tate Liverpool, both related to water – is like a respective manifestation of the process of ripening and decay. *Chandelier* is large, impressive, but has yet to blossom into character. *Boomerang* is a glorious peak of perfection before the rottenness that inevitably follows. *Descending Light* and its predecessor *Fountain of Light* represent monuments to fallen ideals, to bankrupt systems and beliefs. In this sense, where *Descending Light* can be seen as a glittering monument to the decline in values pervading contemporary culture, who needs it to be subtle? It veritably rails against the vulgarity of the age. It parallels the image that inspired it: a scene from a forgotten Soviet film that showed a chandelier poised to fall, swinging fatally from its anchor, shaken by the oncoming revolution that would turn St Petersburg into Leningrad and exterminate the ruling elite. Ai appears to imply that the only way to clean today's slate is to eradicate the debauchery of the reigning elite, a cause to which he donates his expression, using a visual language with which it is most familiar, and as was roundly demonstrated during the two-week run of the Olympic Games in Beijing in August 2008 with the daily tirades delivered via Ai's blog.

Recycling ...

In many of the works discussed so far, the materials used in their construction have been identified as recycled elements of the past: things that are no longer of use themselves, and that would otherwise be cast aside or thrown away. Ironically, across China and most social strata, too, recycling is a long-standing and today highly sophisticated operation, only undermined by the excesses of the socialist embrace of capitalism.

Ai's recycling began in New York: the incorporation of functional objects – shoes, raincoats, bricks, light bulbs, woks, coat hangers – into an artwork constitutes a degree of recycling. A group of 'found' paintings titled *Fifth Street* – named after the location in New York where the paintings were found – was also used to realize a collaborative joke at the expense of the Chinese art world in 1995.[46] Back in China, the recycling began with the furniture works in the late 1990s, but it is most tangible in the examples of the *Map of China* series, *Coffin* (2005),[47] *Template* (2007) and *Kippe* (2006), in which wood from temples was collected and re-used in creative ways: salvaged, reclaimed and seamlessly incorporated into new forms, and to spectacular ends. Ai states that, ironically, 'The wood I use comes from temples destroyed in the name of development, or would be used by antique dealers to make copies of antique furniture.' There is no nostalgia here – rather, a pointed jab at the vulgarity of the present, and the lack of imagination brought to creativity in modern China in the way that these objects are preserved or recycled, cared for or even acknowledged, because, as Ai asserts, 'the people are not free to do and think what they want: to use their imagination'.[48]

Communication

Even before Ai was aware of the technological possibility of a blog, he was firm in his faith that 'Art ought to be a tool, or carriage for conveying information.' He also recognized that 'it changes with the times', as he himself has followed suit, adapting to the times in his embrace of blogging. This is relevant to the discussion because if one had to summarize the goals of Ai's activity, it would have to be in terms of his intention to communicate, or to mediate communication. This is what lends the blog such appeal: it is a means of touching people and moving minds with which Ai would not come into

COFFIN, 2005
IRONWOOD FROM
DISMANTLED TEMPLES OF THE
QING DYNASTY (1644-1911)
37 X 187 X 70 CM
97 X 257 X 130 CM
39 X 278 X 85 CM

FOUNTAIN OF LIGHT, 2007
STEEL AND GLASS CRYSTALS
ON A WOODEN BASE
700 X 529 X 400 CM
INSTALLATION IN PROGRESS
TATE LIVERPOOL

contact in the course of a normal day in the studio. That his blog receives over 10,000 hits a day has encouraged it to become an important element of his creative expression, for as demonstrated with *Fairytale* it is the perfect tool to 'stir the imagination.'

Taking the notion of communication to its logical extreme, in the early 2000s Ai decided never to refuse interviews – until he found himself at siege to the invasion of foreign journalists that travelled to Beijing to cover the Olympics. That notwithstanding, he regularly makes headlines with his acerbic comments. 'I often ask myself why we can't have a society with improved media and no censorship,' he exclaims. 'What have we got to hide? What is so dangerous about the truth?'[49] For one of Ai's generation in China, this is the least creative question, to which the state continues to provide astonishingly creative answers. To that question he must respond.

For Ai, making art is an act of rebellion as well as of communication. The two elements are interwoven and mutually dependent. One could not exist without the other; they are as interdependent as culture, politics and the economics of socialist capitalism in China. Being an artist, in Ai's way of thinking, means confronting these things; only an idiot would pretend not to be affected or claim to see no relevance between them. The question 'What kind of role do you think you could have in China?' is one that Chinese contemporary artists are commonly asked. In the 1990s, Ai would have responded by asking why he should *do* anything for his country, for a society that refuses to acknowledge his existence, which denies progressive art and culture, and discourages a real sense of individualism while continuing to curb its citizens' basic personal freedoms. He would subsequently alter his tone. 'I think I have

the responsibility (it's the first time I use that word) to proclaim life, to be fully aware of what it means. That's a lot to do. To open up possibilities I must be responsible today. Tomorrow could be different.'[50]

Ai's strategy is not without its contradictions. He dips into styles, histories, mediums, tactics and modes of expression at will and as these serve his purpose, such that we might conclude that art is only *part* of the purpose, its mechanism if you like. While Ai clearly takes pleasure in creating, the nature of the agenda he pursues suggests that his interest in advocacy is still stronger than in pure art. Art functions as Ai's personal propaganda. This subversion of art to his life and goals, returns Ai to the sphere of Duchamp, yet given his Chinese heritage, it actually aligns him more closely with the great men of letters through China's long dynastic history, who did not distinguish between 'pictures' or 'words' as functions of the social responsibility they took as their duty in life, and which frequently used both pictures and words as a means of impeaching the state. Ai is the most recent, and successful, in a long line of artistic, or cultural, agents provocateurs. We see this in the ways Ai chooses to navigate the 'moment' (in China, which should be understood as the chaotic momentum of change, a chaos which allows certain possibilities to exist and be utilized) and 'place' (China again, but in the sense of it being a place ruled by a totalitarian regime) to advance dangerous ideas about culture, and the freedoms and responsibilities of the individual. 'You can say nothing is related,' he asserts, 'or that everything is related. I just follow my intuition.' Through words, images, forms and actions, Ai deploys a rich war chest of aesthetic impulses to achieve his goals. The result is an extraordinary body of work that is relevant enough to ensure that the future of art as a whole, not only in China, is that much more radical.

Descending Light
Bernard Fibicher

THE ARTIST PHOTOGRAPHING
TEMPLATE AFTER ITS COLLAPSE,
DOCUMENTA 12, KASSEL, 2007

previous pages,
DESCENDING LIGHT, 2007
GLASS CRYSTAL, LIGHTS, METAL
400 X 663 X 461 CM
INSTALLATION
MARY BOONE GALLERY, NEW YORK,
2008

On the lawn of the Aue-Pavilion during the preview of Documenta 12 (2007) in Kassel stood Ai Weiwei's sculpture Template, a twelve-metre-tall tower constructed from the wooden doors and window frames of Ming and Qing dynasty houses destroyed by the massive building projects that epitomize what I would describe as China's second cultural revolution. But Template was blown down by a violent gust of wind, throwing the exhibition organizers into a panic. Here, after the rice paddy by Sakarin Krue-On and the field of poppies by Sanja Iveković, was yet another outdoor project that was not going according to plan! Ai soon restored calm; not only did he accept the destruction of his installation, but he also proclaimed that he preferred the work in its new state. Perhaps he had no choice? Did he want to show that he was a cool artist? What those unfamiliar with Ai's oeuvre might not have realized was that destruction is a theme that runs through all his work. Indeed, I would even go so far as to characterize it as a fundamental component of his approach. Ai is an iconoclast because the destruction of his system of representation is built into that system itself, as exemplified in two famous series of black and white photographs, one of which documents the artist's ritual destruction of a Han dynasty vase, while the other shows him giving the finger to such symbolically charged public buildings as the White House in Washington and the People's Palace in Beijing. This 'fuck you' gesture is indeed part of the artist's strategy. The collapse of Template thus constituted a natural extension of his work, as if the installation's self-destruction was pre-programmed. Ai had not the slightest problem with the 'fuck you' addressed to him by the collapsing portal, because the event was, so to speak, already planned in his mind.

Ai's iconoclasm is sometimes applied, with great etymological appropriateness, to objects from a religious context (beams and columns from temples assembled to form sculptures, or a Buddha head cut into horizontal slices), but most of the time he uses everyday or symbolic

FOUNTAIN OF LIGHT, 2007
STEEL AND GLASS CRYSTALS
ON A WOODEN BASE
700 X 529 X 400 CM
INSTALLATION
TATE LIVERPOOL

VLADIMIR TATLIN, MONUMENT TO THE
THIRD INTERNATIONAL, 1919-20

objects rooted in tradition, such as houses, furniture and utensils. This is the context in which we should read his lamps, chandeliers and lanterns, which represent a relatively new theme for him. In 2002, Ai made a six-metre-tall crystal chandelier that looked like an overturned tower or wedding cake (Chandelier, 2002). Mirrors attached to a scaffolding structure surrounding the object multiplied its reflections and its splendour. In 2006, for a show at the Queensland Art Gallery in Australia, the artist produced a giant lamp in the form of a boomerang that was mirrored in a pool of water (Boomerang, 2006). Finally, Fountain of Light, exhibited at the Tate Liverpool in 2007, reproduced the structure of Vladimir Tatlin's Monument to the Third International while transforming that icon of Constructivist, revolutionary art into a banal piece of lighting, and one that furthermore was put in a very precarious position, floating in the Irish Sea, facing Tate Liverpool, and making a constant clicking noise of cheap jewellery as it did so. One of Ai's most recent works goes a bit further, in the degree of iconoclasm, consisting of a monumental red lamp-like object lying on the floor, apparently having fallen there. Its brass mounting appears to be distorted by the violent impact of its fall, but none of the glass crystals are broken. Inside, disregarding the doubly twisted spine of the lamp, shines an unbroken helix of lighted bulbs. The light is working in spite of its fall. The sculpture was built from the start as a twisted object, and its fall is clearly an integral part of its design. It is a figure of decadence in the literal, etymological sense: 'de-cadere' means 'to fall' in Latin, so the term therefore refers to the opposite of progress: Moreover, the spiral of light inside the chandelier repeats and at the same time reverses the ascending line in Tatlin's monument. However, this interpretation turns out to be fallacious and one-sided. The work's title, Descending Light (2007), does not speak of destruction but of a process, and can even be said to indicate dynamism. Something is happening — it may be a downwards movement, but it is movement none the less. The fall, with its fatal and irrevocable consequences, has yet to occur. It seems to be suspended in time – imminent, threatening.

The decisive element in the piece – apart from its unwonted position – is its colour: red, which appears in various symbolic forms throughout Chinese culture. Raise the Red Lantern was the title of a film by Zhang Yimou – who happened to attend the famous Beijing Film Academy during the same years as Ai (and Chen Kaige) – based on Su Tong's novel Raise the Red Lantern, about Songlian, a young woman living in China in the 1920s who is forced to become the fourth wife of Master Chen. She immediately finds herself getting caught up in the plotting and rivalry between the other concubines living in his house, the aim being to win the red lantern that indicates the Master's favour, and thus power in the house. Raise the Red Lantern is a film about the colour red. In twentieth-century China, red was the colour of progress and revolution (as evidenced in the Red Guard, Little Red Book and red flag). But in pre-Revolutionary China, it was the symbol of pleasure, desire, happiness, plenitude and luck. Red was the colour of the bride's garments, of the walls of the Forbidden City, of the lanterns made in Gaocheng that people lit up on public squares and in streets during the feats of Shang Yuan on the fifteenth day in the first month of the Chinese New Year. Today, elaborate chandeliers are part of the décor in luxury hotels and restaurants. Whatever the context, this kind of lighting always signifies splendour and celebration. But now this multivalent symbol – with its contradictory allusions to successive imperial and then communist and then consumerist times – is lying on the ground: the party is over, there is no longer anything to celebrate. And yet there remains our fascination with the ruin, with the elegance of the curves sketched in by the cut glass, with the shards of red evoking warmth and sensuality. In Zhang's film, the red lantern hanging outside one of the concubines' houses is the sign of the sexual favours that she is enjoying from Master Chen. Ai is a fervent admirer of Marcel Duchamp, for whom everything was sexualized, and his red lamp is a thinly disguised erotic metaphor. It is impossible not to see this as a Duchampian Objet-dard (Dart-Object) – a huge, tired member – the opposite of the vigorous ceramic urinating figure in Ai's Pee (2007), a heavy, slumped creature struggling to straighten up. This is the interpretation that comes to mind when one looks at the work from a distance, from a fixed viewpoint – when

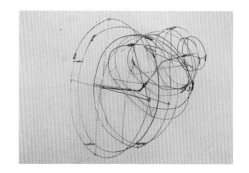

DESCENDING LIGHT MODEL, 2007
WIRE
20 X 33 X 20 CM

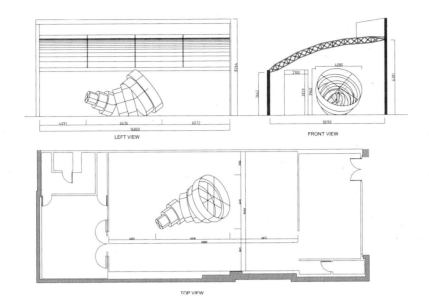

LEFT VIEW

FRONT VIEW

TOP VIEW

one looks at it as an image. But as soon as one begins to confront the sculpture physically and move around it, one realizes that the chandelier that is wide open to our sight is also an enormous uterus engorged with blood in which luminous spermatozoa are moving around, making their way down to the bottom in the hope of a fertile encounter. The chandelier, an object both male and female, is thus not only a sign of impotence, but also a promise of something to come, of a nascent hope. Might this object be a metaphor for Chinese society, Ai's vision of which, as we know, is not very optimistic, to the point of being sometimes frankly disillusioned?

One doesn't have to be a Sinologist in order to understand Chinese contemporary art that is conceived for a global public. Although these artists' work clearly displays the signs of its origins and plays with notions of 'Chinese-ness', they aim to plug into a more extensive, if not universal, system of reference. It is perfectly fair to perceive works from China in the light of our Western culture. In Europe the lantern is a 'beacon' of the Enlightenment. Signifying knowledge and truth, it is the antidote to obscurantism in all its forms. Its use for this symbolic end goes back to antique philosophy: Diogenes, it is said, used to walk through the streets of Athens in the middle of the day carrying a lit lantern. When people questioned him, he informed them that he was looking for a man – thereby implying that the men around him did not behave as true men. The title of Ai's work, Descending Light, indicates the subjacent presence of this metaphoric meaning. The light will come down to us, the truth will out. Will this lamp, like Diogenes' lantern, foster knowledge or awareness? Then again, awareness of what? There is no clear answer to this question. Awareness of the end of something, to be sure. Although he gives us light,

the artist's light does not go everywhere: he leaves some areas in shade, and does not give us all the truth. As the son of one of the major Chinese poets of the twentieth century, who was exiled to the countryside during the Cultural Revolution and later rehabilitated, and having himself lived in the USA for some ten years and taken a critical view of his country's recent development, Ai is wary of truths; his attitude is that of a sceptic who knows all about the inconstancy of phenomena and the subjective relativity of perception.

Descending Light is a paradoxical object: a falling and fallen chandelier, horizontal rather than vertical, collapsed but still in working order, majestic in its decadence, splendid and fragile, sensual and revolutionary red, impotent and erectile, male and female, revealing and mysterious, symbolic and hermetic. It is an object within which, in keeping with his method, the artist has managed to integrate critical distance – a true dialectical object that at once affirms things and their opposite, and that therefore eschews any kind of synthesis. By incorporating destruction into his practice, Ai creates works of art that are almost literally open: fragments, rupture, ambiguity and irony undermine any attempt to form a coherent reading and all the tricks of totalizing reason. In this sense, he is one of those Chinese intellectuals who have taken on board both internal and external points of view, and who live between the two. This also makes him a worthy student of Duchamp, who once professed to doubt in himself and in everything, and to never believing in truth in the first place. Coming from an artist, 'fuck you' is a pretty clear message. Ai brings something forwards, then dissociates himself from it. He lets us get by with the uncertainty generated in this fashion. His enormous red lantern or majestic chandelier is an encumbrance. Rather than hanging inaccessibly from the ceiling, it takes up space on the floor. It is cast down at our feet and thus becomes a project in the very literal sense of the word (from the Latin 'pro-icere', meaning 'to throw forward'. The word has spatio-temporal connotations and implies a process: throwing, from a certain point, towards a target located ahead). It becomes 'our' project. 'Etant donné' ('given') is a trick. With Ai Weiwei, as with Marcel Duchamp, nothing is ever given.

TRANSLATED FROM FRENCH BY CHARLES PENWARDEN

时代－艾青, 1941

我站立在低矮的屋檐下
出神地望着蛮野的山岗
和高远空阔的天空,
很久很久心里象感受了什么奇迹,
我看见一个闪光的东西
它象太阳一样鼓舞我的心,
在天边带着沉重的轰响,
带着暴风雨似的狂啸,
隆隆滚辗而来……

我向它神往而又欢呼！
当我听见从阴云压着的雪山的那面
传来了不平的道路上巨轮颠簸的轧响
我的心追赶着它, 激烈地跳动着
象那些奔赴婚礼的新郎
一纵然我知道由它所带给我的
并不是节日的狂欢
和什么杂耍场上的哄笑,
却是比一千个屠场更残酷的景象,
而我却依然奔向它
带着一个生命所能发挥的热情。

我不是弱者一我不会沾沾自喜,
我不是自己能安慰或欺骗自己的人
我不满足那世界曾经给过我的
一无论是荣誉, 无论是耻辱
也无论是阴沉的注视和黑夜似的仇恨
以及人们的目光因它而闪耀的幸福
我在你们不知道的地方感到空虚
我要求更多些, 更多些呵
给我生活的世界
我永远伸张着两臂
我要求攀登高山
我要求横跨大海
我要迎接更高的赞扬, 更大的毁谤
更不可解的怨恨, 和更致命的打击一
都为了我想从时间的深沟里升腾起来……

没有一个人的痛苦会比我更甚的一
我忠实于时代, 献身于时代, 而我却沉默着
不甘心地, 象一个被俘虏的囚徒
在押送到刑场之前沉默着
我沉默着, 为了没有足够响亮的语言
象初夏的雷霆滚过阴云密布的天空
抒发我的激情于我的狂暴的呼喊
奉献给那使我如此兴奋, 如此惊喜的东西
我爱它胜过我曾经爱过的一切
为了它的到来, 我愿意交付出我的生命
交付给它从我的内体直到我的灵魂
我在它的前面显得如此卑微
甚至想仰卧在地面上
让它的脚像马蹄一样踩过我的胸膛

Shi Dai (Era), 1941

I stand beneath the low eaves
Gazing spellbound at the wild hills,
The lofty, spacious sky.
Long, long ago, in a miracle of the mind
I saw something flashing light;
Like the sun, it inspired me,
At the horizon, a heavy rumble,
The howling of a tempest,
Booming toward …
I face it, rapt, calling out
When, from the dark clouds pressing the snowy peaks, I hear
the sound of giant wheels rolling, bumping down the uneven road
like so many bridegrooms rushing off to weddings

Even if I knew that what it brought me
Was not the fervour of some festival
nor the laughter of a pageant,
but a scene more brutal than a thousand slaughterhouses,
I still rush toward it
with the enthusiasm only life can bring.
I am not among the weak, Nor am I self-content,
I can neither console nor deceive myself
I am not happy with what the world has given me
Not the honour, not the shame
And whether it be the attentive gaze of the heavy clouds above,
or the hatred of a black night
Or the happiness that shines from people's eyes on its account
I, in this place you know not, feel empty.

Give me the living world
I forever extend my arms
I must climb the high mountains
I must cross the vast oceans
I need to hear loftier praise, more damning slander
More inexplicable complaints, and more deadly attacks
All have made me want to rise up from the deep gulf of time …

No one's troubles have been more thorough than mine
I am true to my era, gave myself to it, but I kept silent
Not resigned to it, like a convict taken captive
My silence that of a man being delivered to his execution
I am silent, for lack of sufficient resounding language
Like an early summer thunderbolt rolling through a sky dense with clouds
Unleashing my passion in a violent shout
Directed at that which has made me so excited, so surprised
My love for it greater than all I have ever loved
Willing to hand over my life to hasten its arrival
To hand over to it everything from my body to my soul
Before it I seem so very vulgar
Wishing to lie prone on the ground
Allowing its feet to run ragged over my chest, like a horse upon a road.

么被抹去。迎是一次道义的胜利。在一个民权、民众知情众被列困难的国家，在一个公民舆论媒体缺少基本良知和反思的国家、在一个……文化领导、政府说什么是什么、思川赏到的国家、迎是一个伟大的生利。它说明了在……今天的时代、一切……事实变相

了。公安无权滥用职权、非法
拘留这样一个技术人员和设计、
而任其真正主犯逍遥法外、
这是犯法的，同样是对法律的羞辱。
再者，这样的公案，为什
么不能公开的听证，而是一
切均在秘密之中进行，在
这是要维护、掩饰什么，这
样的公正是公正的吗，还是
离公平和正义更远了呢？

China still lacks a modernist movement of any dimension. For the basis of such a movement is the liberation of humanity and the victory of the humanitarian spirit. Democratic politics, material wealth and universal education are the soil upon which modernism exists, for a developing nation these remain ideals to pursue.

Modernism is a philosophy, a worldview, and a lifestyle. At its core is the questioning of classical thought and critical reflection on the human condition. Any cultural or artistic activity that does not belong to modernism is shallow, lacking in spiritual value. As for the numerous creations that appear modernist but in fact turn their back on the spirit of modernism, these are but superficial imitations.

Modernism has no need of various masks or official titles, it is the primal creation of the awakened, its ultimate concern is with the the meaning of existence and reality of situations. It is vigilance against social and human crises, it is not compromising, it does not cooperate.

Such awakening is reached through a process of self-recognition, a process teeming with a thirst for and pursuit of a spiritual world, with unending doubts and puzzlement.

The result of such fearless truth is that we may observe in modernist works an unadorned authenticity, panic, emptiness and anomia. This is not some cultural choice, just as life is not a choice. It all stems from an interest in one's own existence, this interest is the cornerstone of all spiritual activities, and the goal of all knowledge.

Reflections on modes of existence and spiritual values are core issues in modern art. This is a proactive reflection on the straightforward and distinct facts – the inevitability of life and death, a hollow, boring sense of reality that remains in the processes after primal impulses have passed.

All of this moves towards an inevitable conclusion: an understanding of the solemnity and absurdity of life. We cannot avoid this recognition, just as we cannot avoid the reality of our own existence.

Our dreams are a combination of real limitations on life and our eager impulse to surmount these limitations. Such impulses, and the efforts we spend working towards this goal are the pleasures of life.

Humans are destined to be narrow-minded empiricists. But only by venerating the mystical world can we rise above our petty quandaries. Humans are are animals who have renounced nature, and from

among every possible path, humans have chosen the longest and most remote path leading to the self.

Making choices is how the artist comes to understand himself. These choices are correlated to one's spiritual predicament, and the goal is a return to the self, the pursuit of spiritual values and the summoning of spirits. These choices are inherently philosophical.

A painful truth of today is that even as we import technologies and lifestyles, there is no way to import spiritual awakening, justice or strength. There is no way to import the soul.

Modern Chinese cultural history is precisely a history of negating the value of the individual; it is a soulless history of suppressing humanity. Intellectuals are invariably attacked from all directions. Deemed the representatives of either aggressive forces of Western culture or outdated, feudalistic modes of consciousness, Chinese intellectuals have been put in an embarrassing predicament.

All reform efforts over the past hundred years have begun with a dependence on outside cultures, and they all conclude by coming to terms with native traditions. These simple emulations and ineffective resistances have amounted to an important characteristic of China's modern cultural

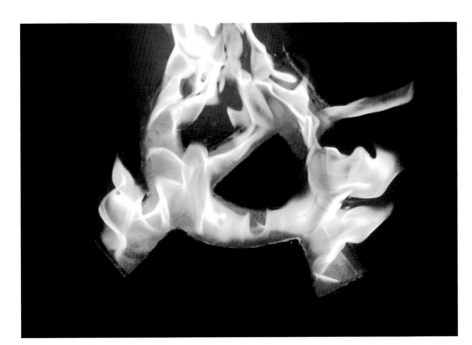

UNTITLED, 1994
PLASTER, DOLLAR BILLS, GAS
40 X 40 CM

development: abandoning intuitive knowledge and selling one's soul in the face of despotism, all in exchange for the right to linger on in a steadily worsening situation.

Without a doubt, the tides of history are pulling this archaic ship ever nearer to the shores of democracy. Communication, identification, understanding, and tolerance have begun to supplant methods of compulsion and exclusion; the new people will live win a happier space, a place of greater intelligence.

Humanity realizes that cultural and spiritual totalitarianism and exclusionism has rendered people's spirits deflated, rendered their wills shrunken, rendered their vision myopic.

Burying troublesome opinions and evading difficult questions is nothing less than scepticism and denial of the value of life. Such behaviour is a blaspheming of gods, an acknowledgement of ignorance and backwardness, a blatant expression of support for unchecked power and injustice.

Today's Chinese culture and art still lack the most basic of concerns – artists lack any sense of understanding of their social position, and fail to deliver independent criticism.

No manner of linguistic exploration, no possible appropriation of strategy or medium, no copying of style or content can mask the flaws of artists when it comes to self-awareness, social critique, and independent creation. These expose a philistine style of pragmatism and opportunism. They reflect impoverished spiritual values and a general lowering of our tastes.

Only when the close attention paid to 'trends' is diverted to personal methods and issues, when explorations of form become explorations into being and spiritual values, will art be somewhat enlightened – such a very long road.

TRANSLATED FROM CHINESE BY PHILIP TINARI

FROM THE GREY BOOK, NOVEMBER 1997

Widespread Beliefs, 2006

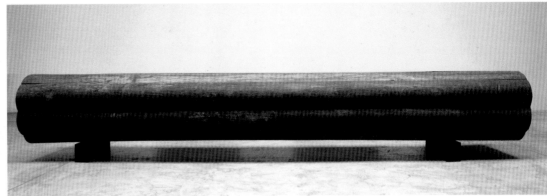

A Worn-out Ship Travelling Over the Seas

Anyone who has seen the ocean knows, it's only a damaged, floating ship, a destination-less, lousy ship that set off from its homeland with its accursed fate, and is forever unable to return home, it will never reach its destination. To where is it sailing? What is its fate or that of its passengers? The price will be no more and no less than the fate of these passengers' emotions and reality. Its fate was predestined decades ago, a hundred years ago: this ship will not travel in bright and glorious channels, but will be shrouded in the interminable darkness of decline, shame and evil conduct. It will be a ship that violates the common ideals and the fate of mankind, floating on gloomy waters. Or perhaps, this is not a ship; it has no captain, no passengers, no direction and no destination. It is merely an object afloat; it cannot even sink, but can only wait for a tempest to tear it to pieces.

National Honour

If national honour exists, it is only something that autocrats busy themselves with ruining. The alleged people are the simple loafers who linger in a steadily worsening situation, those who have been dulled and forsaken by the deceptions of culture, personalities that have been deprived and lost, people who have abandoned their rights and responsibilities. They are the people who walk like ghosts on the widening streets, whose true emotions, dreams and homes are already long lost, who have no warmth in the night, no expectations, and who will not dream again.

The People

They are the crudest, simplest thing on earth. The idea of being the 'master of one's own affairs' or a 'representative of advancement' has become a mere joke that reveals the sensibilities and determination of the dictatorship, the ingratiation of the instinctual lowly slaves. The rights of people, anything that might be called a right, necessarily originate from the self-identification and expression of worth of those who possess them. Rights are necessarily a part of the individual's life force and their awareness; the term inevitably implies they are god-given. There is no person who can bestow rights on others, just as there is no sunless day, and no such thing as a night where the sun hangs high in the sky. In this sense, why are people willing to believe such lies?

Undying Nation

When can we call a nation an 'undying nation'? What are the right kinds of sovereigns or subjects needed to establish this unassailable status, a place with no crises, no hindrances, and no possibility of decline? It must be a land lacking in truth, lacking in justice, a paradise without a soul; and it must unanimously break faith with its people. This is by no means hard to achieve, for this has long been a reality on this piece of land. In this respect, it already possesses some sacred attributes, because of its consummate independence from the evolution of human universal values and laws, the lack of good or evil, willpower, choices, and that destiny itself refers merely to a state of otherness.

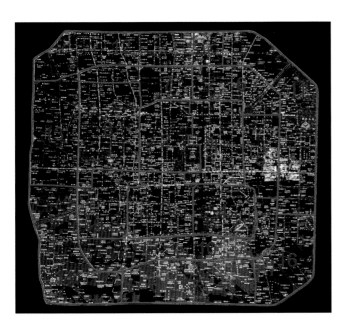

Widespread Beliefs

Here, there is no end to the extremes of corruption and degradation; ignorance and deceit have a power that is hard to resist. People generally believe that individual consciousness is the most useless of social ideals; they believe that fate entails resigning oneself to their situations and hardships, patiently compromising their way through an arbitrary life. A society that lacks individual consciousness is truly gloomy and cold. Such widespread abandonment can cause the very last green leaf to wither; it can extinguish the very last candle. Cherishing your life, restoring its original value, and insisting on individual consciousness are the only true possibilities for existence. All through life, these are the unassailable, inexhaustible source of vitality, these are your protective gods, and they will warm you and illuminate your surroundings. Defending individual consciousness safeguards the thoughts and ideas of others and society, it is the pursuit of truth and a grateful attitude towards beauty. Once a person awakens to their individual consciousness, things have already begun to change.

Conception of History

In today's world, what kind of people have no conception of history? What kind of people would believe that humanity would abandon its natural instinct to pursue beauty, or that the rights and interests of a nation and its people could be permanently devoured by stupidity and humiliation? Who would believe that the power or status of the collective exceeds truth and good will, or that reality would eternally resign itself to falsehoods, that wisdom would forever remain inaccessible, or that aesthetic perception would yield to repulsiveness? What sort of people desire to be bound together in selfish interests, losing their conscience in the process? At the very least, they are shortsighted. This is shortsightedness preserved over several decades, at the cost of the lives of several generations. It is a shortsightedness that turns the fate of the state and nation into a vehicle for pursuing the gains of a few individuals or of the ruling party. To the universe, this is merely a tiny tragedy of a small portion of people; but in a twinkling, this will become the past, something to be held in contempt for later generations. This is because these folks lack accurate understandings of the world and history.

Personal Accomplishments

The combined successes of an individual or a party are never enough to serve as a guide to our virtue, in the event that such success is unrelated to the pursuit of truth or the happiness of others.

TRANSLATED FROM CHINESE BY LEE AMBROZY AND PHILIP TINARI

POSTED ON THE ARTIST'S BLOG, 20 NOVEMBER 2006

We have nothing

Once, at a dinner, I made the comment that we live in the era most lacking in creativity, but that comment was made rather hastily. I almost never use the word 'creativity', rather, I am more inclined to use fantasy, suspicion, discovery, subversion, or criticism, words whose accumulated capacity, in my opinion, define creativity. These are the fundamental requirements of, the very substance of life. They are indispensable.

Creativity is the power to reject the past, to change the status quo, and to seek new potential. Simply put, aside from using one's imagination – and perhaps more importantly – creativity is the power to act. Only through our actions can expectations for change become reality, and only then can our purported creativity build a new foundation, and only then is it possible to draw out human civilization.

Yet, we do not belong to such an era, or to put it another way, we live in a world apart from others who exist in the same era.

It's true. We live in a time that writes off creativity and poisons it to death. When creativity is so formulaically included in every official article and every advertising catch phrase, everyone knows we are living in precisely a despairing time deficient in, most lacking in imagination. Politics are far removed from the common ideals of human society and universal values. There is no other political party that would sever itself from the land that it survives on,

that could so lack intuition and ability, that could so pathetically place the enrichment of a few above the state and the nation.

A country that rejects truth, refuses change, and lacks the spirit of freedom is hopeless; freedom of expression is one of life's basic rights, freedom of expression and understanding are the very cornerstone of civilization. Freedom of speech is just a part of the spirit of freedom – it is one of life's virtues, the very essence of our natural rights. Without freedom of speech there can be no modernity, only a barbaric world.

Over the past decades, this land has been rife with various struggles, overwhelmed by endless political movements; it has teemed with inhuman persecution and death. There has been only the ceaseless corruption of rights, inaction and abandonment, moral perfidy, lack of conscience and the abandonment of hope. Nothing else has changed, as if nothing has happened at all. In such a country, with such a people, under a system that controls the production of culture such as this, what could we possibly have to say about creativity?

Our Ministry of Culture is the furthest removed from culture the entire world over, a bureaucratic apparatus that, culturally speaking, has never once offered any semblance of a contribution; the Writer's Association, the Artist's Association, the painting institutes … they all cultivate their individual respect and live in privilege, living off the fruits of another's

labour. They embody all of society's hypocrisy and fraud; they are not only culturally outdated, they have no creativity, a fact that they themselves are incapable of realizing.

In this respect, the world is equal, near perfect equilibrium. Let those totalitarian rulers, those rich and heartless people, those with no volition or conscience who spend their lives double-crossing and desecrating, let them use their barbarous means to gain the wealth and power they so lust after. What will never belong to them is the trust that comes with honesty, the hope that comes with creation, or the happiness that democracy brings. No matter how abundant your riches, and regardless of your finesse or status, neither you nor your progeny will ever know such pleasures or expectations.

What you can have is a pack of muddle-faced, gold-digging, foolishly giggling 'friendlies': all the dragon-related nightmares you can handle, and year after year of the putrid mouthpiece that is the Spring Festival New Year's television special, hysterical and despicable forced smiles lacking in any decent intentions, and shamefully meaningless, extravagant celebrations.

Because it is simple: this is a land that rejects freedom of both life and of spirit, rejects fact, and fears the future – a land without creativity.

TRANSLATED FROM CHINESE BY LEE AMBROZY AND PHILIP TINARI

POSTED ON THE ARTIST'S BLOG, 30 JANUARY 2008

STUDY OF PERSPECTIVE:
REICHSTAG, 1995-2003
BLACK AND WHITE
PHOTOGRAPH
90 X 127 CM

STUDY OF PERSPECTIVE:
TIANANMEN, 1995-2003
BLACK AND WHITE
PHOTOGRAPH
90 X 127 CM

Edited Conversations

The vast majority of the time, when confronted with the desire to discuss or understand the truth of the matter, intuition tells us this is impossible. This is a lasting grievance that afflicts this group of people.

Evading anything that touches on the fundamental elements and contradictions that make up the present situation and avoiding responsibility are, ostensibly, in order to benefit those in control. However, both are obviously contradictory to reason, because it is only when the truth of a situation is exposed completely that effective solutions naturally emerge. Likewise, only when this natural emergence is not desired can the true facts be concealed. For a long time now, the actual facts surrounding all important events have been concealed and contorted, it is impossible to lay such truths bare before the public.

There is a habitual lack of self-confidence and a weakness at work here, as well as a mechanical mode of self-protection and precaution. The result is public society's mistrust of power itself, and a widespread scepticism that a legitimate mode of power even exists. Today, democracy and justice are no longer simple political ideals; throughout man's struggle for existence they have been proven to constitute an effective praxis benefiting the advancement of the majority. To use various excuses to postpone or delay the course of democracy, or to stay the emergence of a civil society, is to gamble with a people and a nation, all for the temporary profit of a fraction of the population. It is very easy to see through this.

An ideal civil society will resist and eliminate the will of centralized power; it will pin down and fragment power structures. Limited political rights in China results in consortiums, labour unions, and religious organizations with no real significance. Without a balance or restrictions on power structures, without dissident voices, everything is a return to the Soviet era, leading to absolute corruption and impotence. Civil rights are laid to waste and a culture of ideals has collapsed, thus resulting in the fact that when confronted with competition, it is impossible to sustain the courage, responsibility, ideals and identity that such a large nation ought to possess.

Only when individual dignity is consistent with human interests and values, can such emotions come to be known as so-called 'patriotism'. This entails a degree of difficulty. When the interests of nation or groups fail to meet with mankind's common values and social ideals, in the very least, they can be considered parochial and unwise. In this world, absolutely independent interests are already non-existent, and no portion of mankind can exist in isolation. The plight of an individual's existence is inextricably linked to the values of others. Narrow-minded patriotism derives from myopia and shame; it has its basis in a lack of understanding. The concepts of nation, people and rulers must not be confused, for to confuse them would be to pollute the honour of the country, to plagiarize and betray public rights and will.

When the criticism of others touches on sensitive spots, some claim that the feelings of the Chinese people are insulted; but in terms of both linguistic logic and real-life practice, this phrase sounds infantile, causing the so-called 'Chinese' to seem even more like mindless, resentful boors. If, in fact, the citizens of China possessed some manner of collective sentiment, this would more likely reflect something of the jumble of affairs that surround each of them and affect enduring harm on their emotions; for example: a social system declining into despair, the trampling of civil rights, a worsening of the ecosystem, a lagging educational system, the corrupt impotence of officials . . . in this world nothing is bigger, or more enduring that could be more injurious to the feelings of the Chinese people – if someone really cared, if indeed the Chinese people still have feelings.

JUNKYARD IN A BEIJING SUBURB, C. 2000

MONUMENTAL JUNKYARD, 2006
MARBLE
40 PIECES, EACH 213 X 91 X 6 CM
20 PIECES, EACH 210 X 80 X 6 CM
INSTALLATION
LEWIS GLUCKSMAN GALLERY, CORK

In the end, this society finds itself in an awkward and panicked position owing to cultural weakness, asymmetric concepts, and opaque information. A lack of transparency, of scrutinizing public opinion, and a shortage of public channels for communication and a rational cognizance, makes for deviant and contorted policies. It is difficult to assess their ultimate expense.

Any system has the potential to err. But when a system knows only error and every one of its responses are aberrations, we should be conscious of our relationship to reality, of the accuracy of facts, the rationality of language, and the effectiveness of issues. If these problems are not solved – be they international or domestic – they will be permanently dislocated. Lacking an articulated system of values, this system has no means for reacting to real changes, or to collisions of different value systems. It distorts all the pleas for worth that are embodied in each new possibility.

Pointed criticism aids the advancement of society and works towards its transparency and impartiality. The opposite of this is CCTV, that deformed mouthpiece, that no one believes to be impartial or of good intentions. Its distorted facts and fraudulent public opinions are clearly a publicity programme for political principles; it is not what a modern society needs. This kind of media threatens with its power, deceiving and misleading us into believing in society's progress. It also bears unshakable responsibility for these crimes – history will make this clear. When any of these people criticizes the 'false statements' of another country or person, be it the Dalai Lama's government in exile or foreign imperialists, they none the less block out the most damning parts of the original statements, the genuine face and intention of their critiques, using all manner of shady and underhanded means.

In a society that dodges contradictions and cannot make a plausible defence for itself, no public topic can permit even the most basic discussion, and the answers inevitably disappear within an enormous black hole.

When the rights and the will of the people are limited to such an extreme degree, any expression of those rights or that will comes to be seen as either a threat to power or the outcome of unseemly social factors. A longstanding lack of restrictions on power itself, along with a lack of criticality as to the legitimacy of power has led to awkward policies and situations. Having ruled out all other possibilities, those in charge either do not act, or they act wrongly. It's impossible to say how much longer this power structure can be preserved. We only know that the two basic questions of the legitimacy of power and the appropriate use of power have been neither answered nor bypassed, not in thirty years of opening and reform, not in sixty years of the New China.

The circumstances we face today are culturally determined, stemming from basic values and tendencies in Chinese thinking. As society has changed, and as China has abandoned the possibility of self-sufficiency and isolation, people have come to understand this ever more clearly. The sole path to dignity and cultural authority lies in a new understanding of the possibilities and demands of development, a recognition of today's common values, and the pursuit of a new system of spiritual civilization. When a government admits that it is merely one player in a larger drama of social and historical progress, it will begin to treasure all words of criticism. Any government that rejects democratic rights and the will of the people can only be described as a criminal government. That a government like this can keep on going even given the speed and structure of overall global development in today's world is cause for endless amazement.

In the end it matters little whether an individual's viewpoints are tenable or not. Here we are discussing the living conditions and the possibilities of a group of people; and as a tiny fraction of this group, every person possesses not only this obligation, but this privilege.

TRANSLATED FORM CHINESE BY LEE AMBROZY AND PHILIP TINARI

POSTED ON THE ARTIST'S BLOG, 10 JULY 2008

SURVEY Pages 043–111

1   Ai Weiwei interviewed by Giancarlo Politi and Andrea Bellini, 'Planet China', *Flash Art*, no. 252, January-February 2007.

2   Unless otherwise indicated, all quotations from the artist used here were recorded directly by Karen Smith at various periods between 2005 and 2008, in the course of preparing this text, as well as previously producing catalogue essays for the exhibitions 'The Real Thing, Contemporary Art From China' at Tate Liverpool (2007) and 'Illumination' at Mary Boone Gallery, New York (2008). In addition, research was undertaken for several articles published through the same period in various art magazines.

3   Charlie Finch, 'Not So Wei Out', *Artnet.com*, 18 March 2008. The review refers to 'Illumination', Mary Boone Gallery, New York, 8 March-26 April 2008. Ai previously presented two solo exhibitions in New York: 'Old Shoes, Safe Sex' at Art Waves in March 1988, and more recently at Robert Miller Gallery, 9 September-9 October 2004.

4   Ai Weiwei interviewed by Karen Smith, 'Where Architects Fear to Tread', *Art India*, April 2008, p. 59.

5   Ai/Smith, 2008.

6   Ai Weiwei interviewed by Jonathan Watts, 'Ai Weiwei, Designer of the Olympic Stadium', *The Guardian*, 9 August 2007.

7   Due to the scale of *Fairytale Project* and the response of the international press and art media to it, the centrality of the siting of *Template* at Documenta 12, Kassel, and equally following the artist's response to its dramatic collapse during a fierce thunderstorm.

8   Ai/Smith, 2008.

9   David Sylvester, *About Modern Art*, revised edition, Pimlico, London, 2002, p. 18.

10 Politi and Bellini, op. cit.

11 Ai/Smith, 2008.

12 Ibid.

13 Ibid.

14 Universities had ceased to function during the Cultural Revolution (1966-76). When Deng Xiaoping finally consolidated his position, China entered what is known as the period of normalization, during which society attempted to reinstate basic norms. The universities began to reopen in 1977, and recruitment drives were implemented. Most courses did not begin until 1978.

15 Karen Smith, 'Ai Weiwei: 21st Century Beijing Man', *Artist Profile*, no. 3, April 2008, p.55.

16 The Stars Painting Group (more familiarly known simply as the Stars) came together as a formal group in 1979. In the same year, two exhibitions were organized – one attracted nearly 200,000 visitors – leading to a series of confrontations with the state. The response of the group's members was to take to the streets (on National Day in 1979) brazenly parading banners that read 'We Demand Democracy and Artistic Freedom'. The twelve principle members were Huang Rui, Ma Desheng, Yan Li, Wang Keping, Yang Yiping, Qu Leilei, Mao Lizi, Bo Yun, Zhong Ahcheng, Shao Fei, Li Shuang and Ai Weiwei, most of whom had no formal art training. In addition to the art exhibition, the group organized discussions and public poetry readings, often of a deliberately political timbre. The group disbanded in 1983 – some such as Ai Weiwei were already gone – and by 1986, all but one lived abroad.

17 In the early post-Mao era through the late 1970s and early 1980s, although examples of experimental art can be found, the academies taught a rigid academic curricula, that conformed to technical excellence and figurative realism. The painter Wu Guangzhong challenged this status quo in the early 1980s by suggesting that the beauty of nature could have similar spiritual benefits. This idea found support among various strata

of the art community keen to take art out of the clutches of propaganda and bring it back to aesthetics.

18 Wu Guangzhong (b. 1919) joined the art academy in Hangzhou to study Chinese and Western painting in 1936. In 1947, he took up a government scholarship at the Ecole Nationale Supérieure des Beaux Arts in Paris. Back in China in 1950, and teaching at the Central Academy in Beijing, he introduced Western art to the students, and came in for heavy criticism for contravening the position of Soviet Social Realism with his 'bourgeois' inclinations. By the time of the Cultural Revolution in 1966, still refusing to give up his preferences, he was banned from painting, and teaching. From 1970 to 1978 he was sentenced to hard labour for his beliefs.

19 Ai/Smith, 2008.

20 Ibid.

21 David Sylvester, op. cit., 'Johns – I, 1964', p. 222.

22 Ai/Smith, 2008.
    Examples being found in the work of Wang Ziwei and Yu Youhan in Shanghai (Li Shan was slightly later), and in that of Wang Guangyi,

23 then based in Wuhan.

24 Ai/Smith, 2008.

25 Ibid.

26 Ibid.
    The five-point star is one of the oldest symbols known to man, having spiritual significance for Christians and pagans alike, universally representing a relationship between the heavens and the natural elements, such as earth, water, fire. Although five-point stars have been calculated as appearing on the national flags of thirty-five countries, Ai Weiwei was primarily aware of its significance in the iconography of Communism, where its military associations are leveraged to emphasize power and

27 disciplined might.

28 Sean Simon, 'Ai Weiwei's heart belongs to Dada', *Artspeak*, 16 March 1988. For a typical impression of the decade: 'Much of American art in the 1980s was shaped by and responded to the consumerism and feel-good conservatism of the Reagan era. In a decade preoccupied with success and image, art got bigger: bigger in scope and ambition (elaborate sets, large casts, and complex narratives for commercial musicals), bigger in theme (epic visions in the works of Neo-Expressionist painters) ... Art also became far bigger as a cultural presence. From twenty-four-hour-a-day media coverage to in-your-face images of pop art, video, and graffiti, art was more immediate, available, and accessible than ever before. The new scale and influence of art suited Americans in the 1980s. With more disposable income than in the 1970s and weary of the pervasive pessimism of that decade, they wanted to enjoy themselves again.
    'In contrast to the reticence and insularity of art influenced by Minimalism and Conceptualism in the 1970s, much art of the 1980s assumed the form of public address – from Jenny Holzer's use of the Times Square news ticker to broadcast elliptical and vaguely threatening strings of text, to Krzysztof Wodiczko's night-time projections of symbolically charged imagery onto the facades of museums, public buildings, and corporate headquarters. [...] Yet painting also returned with a vengeance after languishing in relative obscurity during the 1970s, reasserting all the myths of originality and authenticity that were under attack in the media-based works of the Pictures Generation from the same moment. Painters such as Julian Schnabel and Sandro Chia mixed expressionist brushwork with a panoply of historical references ... The art world expanded accordingly to accommodate the return of saleable art: galleries groomed their "stables" of artists like racehorses, while collectors jockeyed for the inside track on the next big thing, and the auction houses provided a perfect arena

for conspicuous consumption.' Matthew J. Bruccoli and Richard Layman (eds), '1980's The Arts: Overview', *American Decades*, Gale Group Inc.,

29 Farmington Hills, Michigan, 1996.
    Two Artists Jump on Tracey Emin's Bed, a performance enacted during the

30 Turner Prize Exhibition, Tate Gallery, 1999.

31 Adam Jasper, 'Critical Mass: Ai Weiwei', *Art Review*, May 2008, pp. 54-58.

32 Artist's talk, the China Institute, New York, 7 March 2008.

33 Ai/Smith, 2008.

34 Politi and Bellini, op. cit.
    Ai Weiwei interviewed by Karen Smith, 'Ai Weiwei: 21st Century Beijing

35 Man', *Artist Profile*, no. 3, April 2008, p.58.

36 Ai/Smith, 2008.

37 Ibid.
    Art historian and curator, the late Hans van Dijk (1946-2002), and

38 Frank Uytterhaegen, founder of the Modern Chinese Art Foundation.

39 Zhuangzi, 'Inner Chapters', *Worldly Ways*, c. 350 BC.

40 Ai/Smith, 'Where Architects Fear to Tread', op. cit., p. 58.

41 Ai/Smith, 'Ai Weiwei: 21st Century Beijing Man', op. cit., p.59.

42 *Beijing 2003* is a video work about the city in which the artist lives, and its people. Participants include assistants Liang Ye, Yang Zhichao, and the driver Wu. The work took 16 days to complete beginning on 18 October 2003. Starting below the Dabeiyao highway interchange, the vehicle from which the video was shot travelled every road inside the Fourth Ring Road, one by one, covering approximately 2,400 kilometres, and recording 150 hours of footage, before returning to the point of departure below the Dabeiyao highway interchange. Through the windshield, the camera objectively recorded everything that appeared before the vehicle – the city's streets, scenery, motion of the people – through a single lens. The process becomes the meaning of the work. The other video pieces are similar in approach, but vary in methodology and length, Ai/Smith, 2008.

43 Ai/Smith, 2008.

44 This was made painfully clear in 1997, when a Sui dynasty pot that had been carefully decorated with a Coca-Cola log and sent to New York for exhibition at Max Protetch Gallery, was unceremoniously returned, in pieces, and with a note from the director that claimed the pot to be 'fake', which rendered the 'work' invalid. Ai sent the pot to the carbon dating centre at Oxford University. The lab report he received back, not only verified the authenticity of the pot, but suggested it probably belonged to a slightly earlier date than had been imagined. While Ai felt impelled to make his point, the greater issue, which remained unresolved, was who had the right to claim an artwork created by an artist, according to the internationally recognized terms of postmodernism, to be 'fake'?

45 For a full discussion of the use of light in Ai Weiwei's work see *Illumination*, catalogue to the exhibition 'Illumination', published by Mary Boone Gallery, New York, 2008, pp. 23-7.

46 A group of abandoned paintings were coupled with a critical text about the work of another artist and both published in a Chinese art magazine: no one noticed the incongruity.

47 'In Chinese, a coffin is called a *guancai* [棺材]. Chinese words have a double meaning – *guan* also means "high official" [官] and *cai* means "money" [财] or "prosperity". So this [work] deals with today's values and situation,' 'China's New Faces: Ai Weiwei', BBC World Service interview, 3 March 2005.

48 Ai/Smith, 2008.

49 Ai Weiwei interviewed by Mark Siemon, 'Olympisches Lexikon', *Frankfurter Allgemeine Zeitung*, 31 March 2008.

50 Politi and Bellini, op. cit.

CHRONOLOGY: Ai Weiwei, born 1957 in Beijing, lives and works in Beijing.

1978-1980
Ai Weiwei attends Beijing Film Academy

1979
'The Stars' (first exhibition),
NATIONAL GALLERY, Beijing (group)

1980
'The Stars' (second exhibition),
NATIONAL GALLERY, Beijing (group)

1982
ASIA FOUNDATION, San Francisco (solo)

1986
'China's New Expression',
MUNICIPAL GALLERY, New York (group)

'Avant-Garde Chinese Art',
VASSAR COLLEGE GALLERY, Poughkeepsie, New York (group)

1987
'The Stars at Harvard: Chinese Dissident Art',
FAIRBANK CENTER AT HARVARD UNIVERSITY, Cambridge,
Massachusetts (group)

THE ARTIST WITH ALLEN GINSBERG, NEW YORK, 1986

1988
'Old Shoes, Safe Sex',
ART WAVES, New York (solo)

1988
Simon, Sean, 'Ai Weiwei's heart belongs to Dada', <u>Artspeak</u>,
16 March

1989
'The Stars: Ten Years',
HANART GALLERY, Hong Kong, toured to HANART GALLERY,
Taipei (group)

1993
'Chinese Contemporary Art: The Stars 15 Years'
TOKYO GALLERY (group)

1995
'Change: Chinese Contemporary Art',
GÖTEBORG ART MUSEUM, Sweden (group)

'Configura 2: Dialog der Kulturen',
ANGERMUSEUM, Erfurt, Germany (group)

SELECTED EXHIBITIONS AND PROJECTS
1996-2002

SELECTED ARTICLES AND INTERVIEWS
1996-2002

1996
'Begegnung mit China',
LUDWIG FORUM FÜR INTERNATIONALE KUNST, Aachen,
Germany (group)

1997
'A Point of Contact: Korean, Chinese, and Japanese
Contemporary Art',
TAEGU ART & CULTURE HALL, South Korea (group)

1998
'Double Kitsch: Painters from China',
MAX PROTETCH GALLERY, New York (group)

1999
'Innovations Part I',
CHINA ART ARCHIVES AND WAREHOUSE, Beijing (group)

48th VENICE BIENNALE (group)

'Modern Chinese Art Foundation Collection',
CAERMERKLOOSTER, Ghent, Belgium (group)

'Concepts, Colors and Passions',
CHINA ART ARCHIVES AND WAREHOUSE, Beijing (group)

Ai Weiwei Studio House, Caochangdi, Beijing
(architectural project)

2000
'Fuck Off' (selected by Ai Weiwei)
EAST LINK GALLERY, Shanghai (group)

'Our Chinese Friends',
ACC GALERIE and GALERIE DER BAUHAUS-UNIVERSITÄT,
Weimar, Germany (group)

'Portraits, Figures, Couples and Groups',
BIZART, Shanghai (group)

China Art Archives and Warehouse, Caochangdi, Beijing
(architectural project)

Soho New Town, Beijing (landscape design)

2000
Kunz, S., 'Aufbruch in China', Art, no. 5

2001
'Take Part 1 & 2',
GALERIE URS MEILE, Lucerne (group)

'Tu Mu: Young Chinese Architecture',
AEDES GALERIE, Berlin (group)

2001
Robecchi, Michele, 'Chinese Art at the End of the Millennium',
Flash Art, no. 217, March-April

2002
'China: Tradition und Moderne',
LUDWIG GALERIE SCHLOSS OBERHAUSEN, Germany (group)

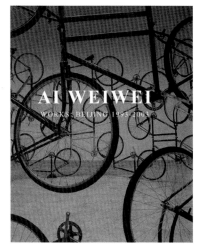

2002 (cont.)
'Art from a Changing World',
HENIE ONSTAD KUNSTSENTER, Hoevikodden, Norway (group)

Bar Jia 55, Beijing (architectural project)

2003
GALERIE URS MEILE, Lucerne (solo)

'New Zone: Chinese Art',
ZACHETA NATIONAL GALLERY OF ART, Warsaw (group)

'A Strange Heaven: Contemporary Chinese Photography',
GALERIE RUDOLFINUM, Prague (group)

'Junction: Chinese Contemporary Architecture of Art,
LIANYANG ARCHITECTURE ART MUSEUM, Shanghai (group)

'Cement: Marginal Space in Contemporary Art',
CHAMBERS FINE ART, New York (group)

Yiwu Riverbank, Jinhua, Zhejiang, China (architectural project)

Jinhua Ai Qing Cultural Park, Jinhua, Zhejiang, China
(architectural project)

Anter Automotive Factory, Huaiyin, Jiangsu, China
(architectural project)

Commune by The Great Wall, Beijing (landscape design)

2003
Lewis, A., 'China Now', South China Morning Post, 3 March

2004
KUNSTHALLE BERN (solo)

CAERMERKLOOSTER PROVINCIAAL CENTRUM VOOR KUNST
EN CULTUR, Ghent, Belgium (solo)

ROBERT MILLER GALLERY, New York (solo)

'Regeneration: Contemporary Chinese Art from China and the US',
SAMEK ART GALLERY, Lewisburg, Pennsylvania, toured to
DAVID WINTON BELL GALLERY, Providence, Rhode Island; JEAN
PAUL SLUSSER GALLERY, Ann Arbor, Michigan; WILLIAMS
MUSEUM OF ART, Williamstown, New Jersey; UNIVERSITY OF
CALIFORNIA SAN DIEGO ART GALLERY, La Jolla; ARIZONA
STATE UNIVERSITY ART MUSEUM, Tempe (group)

'Between Past and Future: New Photography and Video from
China',
INTERNATIONAL CENTER OF PHOTOGRAPHY, New York, toured
to SEATTLE ART MUSEUM; MUSEUM OF CONTEMPORARY ART
and DAVID AND ALFRED SMART MUSEUM OF ART, Chicago;
NASHER MUSEUM OF ART, Durham, North Carolina; SANTA
BARBARA MUSEUM OF ART, California; HAUS DER KULTUREN
DER WELT, Berlin; VICTORIA AND ALBERT MUSEUM, London
(group)

'Chinese Object: Dreams & Obsessions',
SALVATORE FERRAGAMO GALLERY, New York (group)

'Modern Style in East Asia',
BEIJING TOKYO ART PROJECTS, Beijing (group)

'On the Edge: Contemporary Chinese Photography and Video',
ETHAN COHEN FINE ARTS, New York (group)

2004
Colonnello, Nataline, 'Beyond the Checkmate', Art Asia Pacific,
no. 40

Fibicher, Bernard, 'Ai Weiwei', Berner Kunstmitteilungen, no. 342

Hart, Sara, '2008 Beijing Olympics: Innovative Architecture ready
to change the Face on an Ancient City', Architectural Record

Henkes, Alice, 'Ai Weiwei in der Kunsthalle Bern', Kunst
Bulletin, May

Schindhelm, Michael, 'Der gehäutete Volkskörper, Basler Zeitung
Kulturmagazin, 16 October

Spinelli, Claudia, 'Mao am Ende: Chinas Künstler beruhigen
den Besserwestler mit Sozialistenpop. Einer aber erweist sich
als Schlitzohr: Ai Weiwei', Die Weltwoche

THE ARTIST INSTALLING CHANDELIER, GHENT, 2004

2004 (cont.)
'Misleading Trails',
CHINA ART ARCHIVES AND WAREHOUSE, Beijing, toured to
SAMEK ART GALLERY, Lewisburg, Pennsylvania; SCHICK ART
GALLERY, Saratoga Springs, Florida; BOYDEN GALLERY, St
Mary's City, Maryland; FINE ART GALLERY AT VANDERBILT
UNIVERSITY, Nashville; CHARLOTTE AND PHILIP HANES ART
GALLERY, Winston-Salem, North Carolina; UNIVERSITY OF
NORTH TEXAS ART GALLERY, Denton; ALTGELD GALLERY,
DeKalb, Illinois (group)

9th VENICE BIENNALE OF ARCHITECTURE (group)

'Piss Off',
MUSEUM OF NEW ART, Pontiac, Illinois (group)

'Silknet: Emerging Chinese Artists',
GALERIE URS MEILE, Lucerne (group)

'Persona3'
CHINA ART ARCHIVES AND WAREHOUSE (group)

'Le Printemps de Chine',
CENTRE RHÉNAN D'ART CONTEMPORAIN (CRAC), Altkirch,
France (group)

Go Where Restaurant, Beijing (architectural project)

Ya Bar, Beijing (architectural project)

9 Boxes, Thaihot Real Estate, Beijing (architectural project)

2005
2nd GUANGZHOU TRIENNALE, China (group)

'A Strange Heaven: Contemporary Chinese Photography',
HELSINKI CITY ART MUSEUM (group)

'Mahjong: Chinesische Gegenwartskunst aus der Sammlung Sigg',
KUNSTMUSEUM BERN, toured to MUSEUM DER MODERNE,
Salzburg; HAMBURGER KUNSTHALLE, Hamburg; BERKELEY ART
MUSEUM, California (group)

'China as seen by Contemporary Chinese Artists',
SPAZIO OBERDAN, Milan (group)

1st MONPELLIER BIENNIAL OF CHINESE CONTEMPORARY ART,
France (group)

'Convergence at E116/N40',
PLATFORM CHINA CONTEMPORARY ART INSTITUTE,
Beijing (group)

Courtyard 104, Beijing (architectural project)

Courtyard 105, Caochangdi, Beijing (architectural project)

Extension of Studio House, Caochangdi, Beijing
(architectural project)

2005
Spalding, David, 'Dream Factory, Rubbish Heap', Contemporary,
no. 72

Yao, Pauline Jiashan, 'Between Truth and Fiction: Notes on
Fakes, Copies, and Authenticity in Contemporary Chinese Art',
Yishu: Journal of Contemporary Chinese Art, summer

2006
'Fragments',
GALERIE URS MEILE, Beijing (solo)

'Territorial: Ai Weiwei and Serge Spitzer',
MUSEUM FÜR MODERNE KUNST, Frankfurt am Main (solo)

2006
Lu, Heng-Zhong, 'An Interview with Ai Weiwei, one of
the architects of Jinhua Architecture Park, Zhejiang',
Time + Architecture, no. 1

PORTABLE TEMPLE, 2005
BAMBOO WOOD, STAINLESS STEEL
500 X ⌀ 400 CM
OSTEND, BELGIUM, 2006

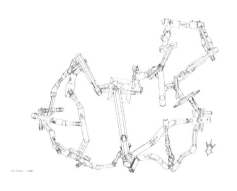

2006 (cont.)
'Cityscapes "Beijing Welcomes You": Ein Stadtmodell von Lu Hao sowie Fotografien von Ai Weiwei',
KUNSTHAUS HAMBURG (solo)

'2006 Beaufort Outside',
MUSEUM OF MODERN ART, Ostend, Belgium (group)

'Art in Motion',
SHANGHAI MUSEUM OF CONTEMPORARY ART (group)

'This is not for you: Diskurse der Skulptur',
THYSSEN-BORNEMISZA CONTEMPORARY ART, Vienna (group)

'China Now: Faszination einer Weltveränderung',
SAMMLUNG ESSL, Klosterneuburg, Austria (group)

15th BIENNALE OF SYDNEY (group)

5th ASIA-PACIFIC TRIENNIAL OF CONTEMPORARY ART,
Brisbane (group)

'Detours: Tactical Approaches to Urbanization in China',
ERIC ARTHUR GALLERY, Toronto (group)

'Altered, Stitched and Gathered',
P.S.1 CONTEMPORARY ART CENTER, New York (group)

'China Power Station I',
BATTERSEA POWER STATION, London (group)

3rd BUSAN BIENNALE, South Korea (group)

'Inspired by China',
PEABODY ESSEX MUSEUM, Salem, Massachusetts, toured to
MUSEUM OF FORT LAUDERDALE, Florida (group)

'China Contemporary: Architecture, Art and Visual Culture',
NETHERLANDS ARCHITECTURE INSTITUTE, Rotterdam (group)

'Black and Blue',
ROBERT MILLER GALLERY, New York (group)

'A Continuous Dialogue',
GALLERIA CONTINUA, Beijing, toured to GALLERIA CONTINUA,
San Gimignano, Italy (group)

2007
'Ai Weiwei',
GALERIE URS MEILE, Lucerne (solo)

'Travelling Landscapes',
AEDESLAND, Berlin (solo)

'EI: Entity Identity - Beijing Series',
STEDELIJK MUSEUM 'S-HERTOGENBOSCH, Netherlands (group)

'Energies-Synergy',
FOUNDATION DE 11 LIJNEN, Oudenburg, Belgium (group)

'Fortunate Objects: Selections from the Ella Fontanals Cisneros Collection',
CISNEROS FONTANALS ART FOUNDATION, Miami (group)

'Inspired by China: Contemporary Furnituremakers Explore Chinese Traditions',

'Branded and on Display',
KRANNERT ART MUSEUM, Champaign, Illinois, toured to ULRICH MUSEUM OF ART, Wichita, Kansas (group)

2006 (cont.)
Colonnello, Nataline, and Huang, S., 'Fragment Conversation between Xiao Ling and Ai Weiwei', Art Today, no. 2

Colonnello, Nataline, 'Figments of Fragments: Ai Weiwei on his first Chinese mainland solo exhibition', That's Beijing, April

Duff, Stacey, 'Capital Comeback: They are two of China's most influential artists but Ai Weiwei and Zhu Wie are yet to have a solo exhibit in their home city', Time Out Beijing, no. 19

Jun, Jun, 'No Frontiers/No Limits: The Artwork of Ai Weiwei', Artco Magazine, May

Münter, Ulrike, 'Die Kunst der Beschleunigung', Berliner Zeitung, 3 May 2006

Obrist, Hans Ulrich, 'Ai Weiwei', Domus, no. 894, July-August

Leanza, Beatrice, 'Ai Weiwei at Galerie Urs Meile, Beijing', Flash Art, no. 249, July-September

Spalding, David, 'Ai Weiwei', Artforum, September

Krueger, J., 'Ai Weiwei'; 'Soul Reversal', Perspective, October

Pollack, Barbara, 'A Bowl of Pearls, a Ton of Tea, and an Olympic Stadium', Artnews, October

Lu, Carol, 'The inflated business of China contemporary art';
David Spalding, 'Guan Yi', Contemporary, no. 80

Tinari, Philip, 'China Power and Chinese Power', Fused Magazine

2007
Politi, Giancarlo, and Andrea Bellini, 'Planet China', Flash Art, no. 252, January-February

Colonnello, Nataline, 'Ai Weiwei: Kippe', Contemporary Art & Investment, no. 1

Lau, P., 'Ein Besuch der Documenta 12, unter Berücksichtigung von Ai Weiwei', Kassels Schlagzeilenproduzent, no. 1

Von Taube, Annika, 'Happily ever after? Will the Documenta change 1001 Chinese lives?', Sleek Magazine, no. 2

Chang, Patty, 'Ai Weiwei', Contemporary Art & Investment, no. 2

Tinari, Philip, 'Made in China: The status symbol in the West is a work of art from the East', New York Times, 25 February

Péus, Camilla, 'Kunstkaiser', Architektur und Wohnen, no. 3

Feng, Boyi, 'Some Remarks on Ai Weiwei', Beijing Art Gallery Magazine, no. 112/13

2007 (cont.),
'China Now',
COBRA MUSEUM, Amsterdam (group)

'Something New Pussycat',
KLARA WALLNER GALERIE, Berlin (group)

'Chinese Video: Chord Changes in the Megalopolis',
MORONO KIANG GALLERY, Los Angeles (group)

DOCUMENTA 12, Kassel, Germany (group)

'Thermocline of Art: New Asian Waves',
ZENTRUM FÜR KUNST UND MEDIENTECHNOLOGIE (ZKM),
Karlsruhe, Germany (group)

'Metamorphosis: The Generation of Transformation in Chinese
Contemporary Art.
TAMPERE ART MUSEUM, Finland (group)

'The Year of the Golden Pig: Contemporary Chinese Art from the
Sigg Collection',
LEWIS GLUCKMAN GALLERY, Cork, Ireland, toured to CENTRO
CULTURAL BANCO DO BRAZIL, Rio de Janeiro (group)

'China Welcomes You ... Desires, Stuggles, New Identities',
KUNSTHAUS GRAZ, Austria (group)

2nd MOSCOW BIENNALE (group)

'Money',
BEIJING TODAY GALLERY, Beijing (group)

'Forged Realities',
UNIVERSAL STUDIOS, Beijing (group)

'The Real Thing: Contemporary Art from China',
TATE LIVERPOOL, toured to INSTITUT VALENCIÀ D'ART MODERN
(IVAM), Valencia (group)

'A Vista of Perspectives',
OCT CONTEMPORARY ART TERMINAL, Shenzhen, China (group)

'Origin Point: The Stars Group Retrospective Exhibition',
TODAY ART MUSEUM, Beijing (group)

'What About Sculpture?',
CHAMBERS FINE ART, New York (group)

Jiangnanhui Seven Villas, Hangzhou, China (architectural project)

Three Shadows Photography Arts Center, Caochangdi, Beijing
(architectural project)

17 Studios, Caochangdi, Beijing (architectural project)

Museum of Neolithic Pottery, Jinhua, Zhejiang, China
(architectural project)

Jinhua Architectural Art Garden, China (curating and landscape
design)

Shulang Factory, Yantai, Shangdong, China (architectural project)

Treehouse of the Waterville, Lijiang, Yunnan, China
(architectural project)

2007 (cont.)
Hosch, Alexander, 'Ai Weiwei: China's Renaissance Man',
Architectural Digest, March

Bork, Henrik, 'Wir bringen unsere eigenen Köche mit', Tages-
Anzeiger, April

Tung, D., 'It's all about Destiny! Isn't It?'; Xiaodong Fu, 'From the
Inside of Life: About Documenta 12', Art China, no. 4

Yao, Pauline Jiashan, 'Ai Weiwei', Contemporary Art & Investment,
April

Tobler, Konrad, 'Manche hatten nicht einmal einen Namen: Der
Luzerner Galerist Urs Meile über die 1001 Chinesen, die für die
Documenta nach Kassel reisen', Berne Sonntags Zeitung, 27 May

Münter, Ulrike, 'Märchen mal anders', Die Tageszeitung, 11 June

Schreiber, Anne, 'Keine Kunst ohne Risiko. Warum Starkünster
Ai Weiwei 1001 Chinesen zur Documenta nach Kassel holt und
was das mit Kultur zu tun hat: ein Experiment mit ungewissem
Ausgang', Handelsblatt, 14 June

Altorfer, Sabine, 'Lieber Träume als Gemurmel. Documenta
12 Kassel. Die Weltkunstausstellung verdient die Bezeichnung
"global". Die Show der Unbekannten hat aber einen heimlichen
Star', Berner Rundschau, 15 June

Maak, Niklas, 'Das Geschenk der Wettergötter. Produktives
Scheitern ist ein Grundmotiv dieser Documenta. Bei Ai Weiwei's
Skulptur hat nun ein Unwetter nachgebessert', Frankfurter
Allgemeine Zeitung, 22 June

Cotter, Holland, 'Asking serious questions in a very quiet voice',
New York Times, 22 June

Bassets, Marc, 'Kassel y el viento creador: El artista chino Ai
Weiwei asegura que su escultura "Plantilla" gana en expresividad
tras su destrucción accidental', La Vanguardia, 24 June

Nav, Haq, 'Yes again, and this time it's for real: An interview with
Simon Groom and Karen Smith', Yishu Journal of Contemporary
Chinese Art, summer

Tinari, Philip, 'A Kind of True Living', Artforum, summer

Blume, Georg, 'Ich habe einen Traum: Ai Weiwei', Zeitmagazin,
26 July

Audédat, Michel, 'L' art c'est aussi du vent', L'Hebdo, 28 June

Aloi, Daniel, 'Ai Weiwei: Smashing China's traditions in art and
architecture', World Literature Today, July

Neidhart, Christoph, 'Der Chinesentransporter', Weltwoche,
22 July

Lorch, Catrin, 'Formvollendeter Allgemeinzustand der Welt:
die Documenta', Kunst Bulletin, July-August

Welti, Alfred, 'Der Kaiser von Kassel', Art, no. 8

Jocks, H. N., 'Ai Weiwei: Das Märchen von 1001 Chinesen. Ein
Gespräch mit Heinz Nobert Jocks', Kunstforum International,
no. 187, August-September

Adam, Hubertus, 'Follies am Flussufer: Jinhua Architectural Park
2004-2006', Archithese, 8 August

Melvin, Sheila, 'Framing Photos as Art in China', Herald
International Tribune, 8 August

'Arts

My tour de force

More than 1,000 Chinese were taken to
Germany to form a unique exhibition by
artist Ai Weiwei, writes David Frazier

A splitting headache in Beijing

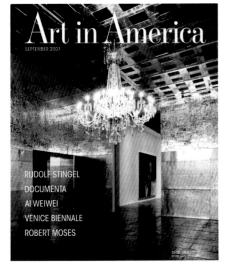

Art in America

SEPTEMBER 2007

RUDOLF STINGEL
DOCUMENTA
AI WEIWEI
VENICE BIENNALE
ROBERT MOSES

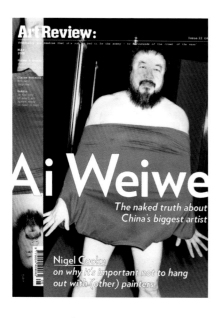

MARY BOONE
GALLERY 541 WEST 24 STREET NEW YORK 10011 (212) 752 2929

08 MARCH – 26 APRIL 2008
AI WEIWEI

RECEPTION FOR ARTIST
SATURDAY 08 MARCH 2008
FROM 5PM UNTIL 7PM

"DESCENDING LIGHT" (WORK IN PROGRESS)
156" BY 180" BY 268", GLASS CRYSTALS/STAINLESS STEEL, ELECTRIC LIGHTS, 2007

AI WEIWEI

MAY 7 - JUNE 1, 2008

The Mayor of of Campbelltown
Councillor Aaron Rule warmly invites you
and your guests to attend the opening of

**Ai Weiwei:
Under Construction**

New commission as part of a major survey exhibition
Curated by Dr Charles Merewether

on Thursday 1 May 7 – 9 pm
to be officially launched
by Chris Hayes, Federal Member for Werriwa

Please RSVP attendance to
artscentre@campbelltown.nsw.gov.au

Exhibition dates: 2 May – 29 June 2008

This exhibition is being held in conjunction
with *Ai Weiwei: Under Construction* at
Sherman Contemporary Art Foundation, curated
by Dr Charles Merewether. The accompanying
full-colour, 160-page catalogue, written by
Dr Merewether and published by UNSW Press in
association with Sherman Contemporary Art
Foundation and Campbelltown Arts Centre
will be available at both venues.

A bus will operate between Sherman
Contemporary Art Foundation and Campbelltown
Arts Centre on the first two Saturdays of the
exhibition (3 May and 10 May) and the first
Saturday of the Sydney Biennale (21 June).

**For bus times or to make a booking,
contact Jaime Wheatley on (02) 9331 1112.
As space is limited, please book early
to avoid disappointment.**

Campbelltown Arts Centre

Corner Camden and Appin Roads, Campbelltown
Sydney NSW 2560 Australia
Phone +61 (02) 4645 4100
Fax +61 (02) 4645 4105

www.campbelltown.nsw.gov.au

arts nsw

SELECTED EXHIBITIONS AND PROJECTS
2008

2008
'Go China! Ai Weiwei',
GRONINGER MUSEUM, Netherlands (solo)

'Ai Weiwei: Illumination',
MARY BOONE GALLERY, New York (solo)

'Ai Weiwei: Under Construction',
SHERMAN CONTEMPORARY ART FOUNDATION and
CAMPBELLTOWN ARTS CENTRE, Sydney (solo)

GALLERY HYUNDAI, Seoul (solo)

ALBION GALLERY, London (solo)

'Red Aside: Chinese Contemporary Art of the Sigg Collection',
FUNDACIÓ JOAN MIRÓ, Barcelona (group)

'Reconstruction #3: The Artist's Playground',
SUDELEY CASTLE, England (group)

'Community of Tastes',
IBERIA CENTER FOR CONTEMPORARY ART, Beijing (group)

5th LIVERPOOL BIENNIAL (group)

'Body Media',
TANG CONTEMPORARY ART, Beijing (group)

11th VENICE BIENNALE OF ARCHITECTURE (group)

'Half-Life of a Dream',
SAN FRANCISCO MUSEUM OF MODERN ART (group)

'Delirious Beijing',
PKM GALLERY, Beijing (group)

'New Vista: The Phenomenon of Post-Tradition in
Contemporary Art',
WHITE SPACE GALLERY, Beijing (group)

'The Real Thing: Contemporary Art from China',
ISTITUT VALENCIA D'ART MODERN (IVAM), Spain (group)

Beijing National Stadium (in collaboration with Herzog & de
Meuron) (architectural project)

SELECTED ARTICLES AND INTERVIEWS
2008

2008
Toy, Mary-Anne, 'The Artist as an Angry Man', The Age,
19 January

Ai Weiwei, 'Influence: Today or Tomorrow', Art Asia Pacific
Almanac, no. 3

Grima, Joseph, 'Ai Weiwei', Icon, no. 57, March

Manonelles Moner, Laia, 'Cómo se rompe un jarrón chino?',
Art & Co, no. 3

Pasternack, Alex, 'Reluctant Return for a Beijing Provocateur',
New York Sun, 7 March

Siemon, Mark, 'Olympisches Lexikon', Frankfurter Allgemeine
Zeitung, 1 April

Smith, Karen, 'Ai Weiwei: 21st Century Beijing Man', Artist Profile,
no. 3, April

Smith, Karen, 'Where Architects Fear to Tred', Art India, April

Ai Weiwei, Amy Cappellazzo, Thomas Crow, Donna De Salvo,
Isabelle Graw, Dakis Joannou, Robert Pincus-Witten, James
Meyer and Tim Griffin, 'Art and its Markets: A Roundtable
Discussion', Artforum, April

'Galleries – Chelsea: Ai Weiwei', The New Yorker, 7 April

Baker, R. C., 'Best in Show: Ai Weiwei "Illumination"', Village
Voice, 9 April

Pollack, Barbara, 'Ai Weiwei Illumination', Time Out New York,
10 April

Jasper, Adam, 'Critical Mass: Ai Weiwei', Art Review, no. 22, May

Vine, Richard, 'The Way We Were, The Way We Are'; Boucher,
Brian, 'Ai Weiwei at Mary Boone', Art in America, June

Lu, Carol, 'Mr. Big', Frieze, June-August

Kelley, Jeff, 'Ai Weiwei: Look Back', Artforum, September

De Muynck, Bert, 'I jumped on the wrong train: Ai Weiwei
looks back on his short but intense career as an architect',
Mark Magazine, no. 12

Colonnello, Nataline, 'Ai Weiwei', Contemporary, no. 96

BIBLIOGRAPHY

SELECTED MONOGRAPHS, EXHIBITION CATALOGUES AND SURVEYS

Ai Weiwei, and Zeng Xiaojun, The Black Cover Book, Red Flag Books, Beijing, 1994

Ai Weiwei, and Zeng Xiaojun, The White Cover Book, Red Flag Books, Beijing, 1995

Ai Weiwei, and Zeng Xiaojun, The Grey Cover Book, Red Flag Books, Beijing, 1997

Ai Weiwei, Hua Tianxue, and Feng Boyi (Eds), Fuck Off, Eastlink Gallery, Shanghai, 2000

Ai Weiwei, Chin-Chin Yap, Charles Merewether and Jonathan Napack, Ai Weiwei Works: Beijing 1993-2003, Timezone 8, Beijing, 2003

Ai Weiwei, J. P. Van der Meiren, Beatrice Leanza, and Carole Lauvergne, Ai Weiwei, Caermersklooster Provinciaal Centrum voor Kunst en Cultuur, Ghent, 2004

Ai Weiwei, Beijing 10/2003, Timezone 8, Beijing, 2005

Ai Weiwei, Chen Weiqing and Nataline Colonnello, Ai Weiwei: Fragments 2006, Galerie Urs Meile and Timezone 8, Beijing, 2006

Ai Weiwei, and Eduard Kögel, Fake Design in the Village, AedesLand, Berlin, 2007

Ai Weiwei, Camille Morineau and Nataline Colonnello, Energies-Synergy, Foundation De Elf Lijnen, Oudenburg, Belgium, 2007

Ai Weiwei, Philip Tinari and Peter Pakesch, Ai Weiwei Works: 2004-2007, Galerie Urs Meile, Beijing, and JRP Ringier, Zurich, 2008

Ai Weiwei, and Karen Smith, Ai Weiwei: Illumination, Mary Boone Gallery, New York, 2008

Ai Weiwei, Gao Minglu, Nataline Colonnello, and Paul Donker Duyvis, Li Zhangyang: Rent Collection Yard, Galerie Urs Meile, Beijing and Lucerne, 2008

Ai Weiwei, Aaron Betsky and Charles Merewether, Ai Weiwei, Albion Gallery, London, 2008

Adrià, Miquel, Alberto Campo Baeza, Kurt Forster, Zaha Hadid, Davina Jackson and Jong-Kyu Kim, 10x10 2, Phaidon, London, 2007

Brewinska, Maria, New Zone. Chinese Art, Zacheta National Gallery of Art, Warsaw, 2003

Buergel, Roger M., and Ruth Noack, Documenta 12, Taschen, Cologne, 2007

Buergel, Roger M., and Ruth Noack, Bilderbuch: Documenta Kassel 16/06-23/09 2007, Taschen, Cologne, 2007

Cavalera, Fabio, Il manager dei bagni pubblici (e altre storie di vita cinese), Rizzoli, Milan, 2007

Clark, John, and Hans van Dijk, Modern Chinese Art Foundation, Osst-Vlanderen, Provincieraad, Belgium, 1999

Clark, John (ed.), Bernell, Robert, Chinese Art at the End of the Millenium, New Art Media Limited, Hong Kong 2000

Costantino, Maria Grazia, Dalu Jones and Filippo Salviati, Arte Contemporanea Cinese, Electa Mondadori, Milan, 2006

Fibicher, Bernard, Feng Boyi, Christoph Heinrich, Pi Li, Uli Sigg, Li Xianting, Hou Hanru and Matthias Frehner, Mahjong: Contemporary Chinese Art from the Sigg Collection, Hatje Cantz, Ostfildern-Ruit, 2005

Folke, Edwards, Foeraendring/Utvlecking, Konsthallen Goetaplatsen, Göteborg, 1996

Gong Mingguang, Art in Motion, Shanghai Shuhua, Shanghai, 2006

Groom, Simon, and Karen Smith, The Real Thing: Contemporary Art in China, Tate Liverpool, 2007

Grosenick, Uta, and Caspar H. Schübbe, China Art Book: The 80 Most Renowed Chinese Artists, DuMont, Cologne, 2007

Gutierrez, Laurent, Valerie Portefaix and Ai Weiwei, MAP Office: The Parrot's Tale, Map Book, Hong Kong, 2008

Hou Hanru, Hans Ulrich Obrist and Guo Xiaoyan, Guangdong Museum of Art: An Extraordinary Space of Experimentation for Modernization, Lingnan Fine Arts, Guangzhou, 2005

Jodidio, Philip, Architecture in China, Taschen, Cologne, 2007

Keller, Samuel (ed.), Art Basel Conversations, Art Basel and Hatje Cantz, Ostfildern-Ruit, 2006

Liu Xiaodong, Ai Weiwei, Britta Erickson and Charles Merewether, Liu Xiaodong: The Richness of Life, Timezone 8, Beijing, 2008

Lu, Carol, et al., Vitamin 3-D, Phaidon, London, 2009

Lü Peng, and Yi Dan, A History of China Modern Art 1979-1989, Hunan Fine Arts, Hunan, 2002

Maltzan, Michael, Richard Armstrong, Raymund Ryan, Ai Weiwei and Mirko Zardini, Michael Maltzan: Alternate Ground, Carnegie Museum of Art, Pittsburg, 2005

Meile, Urs (ed.), Galerie Urs Meile Beijing-Lucerne 2008, Galerie Urs Meile, Beijing, 2008

Merewether, Charles, Zones of Contact, Biennale of Sydney, 2006

Möller, Peter, Configura 2: Dialog der Kulturen, Erfurt, Germany, 1996

Obrist, Hans Ulrich, and Philip Tinari (ed.), HUO: The China Interviews, Office for Discourse Engineering, Beijing, 2009

Pakesch, Peter (ed.), Wang Jing and Lu Chang'an, China Welcomes You ... Desires, Struggles, New Identities, Walther König, Cologne, 2007

Palazzoli, Daniela, Cina: Prospettive d'Arte Contemporanea, Skira, Milan, 2005

Rhee, Wonil, Peter Weibel and Gregor Jansen, Thermocline of Art: New Asian Waves, Hatje Cantz, Ostfildern-Ruit, 2007

Seear, Lynne, Suhanya Raffel (eds) and Sarah Tiffin, The 5th Asia-Pacific Triennial of Contemporary Art, Queensland Art Gallery, Australia, 2007

Shin Yong, and Kim D., A Point of Contact: Korean, Chinese, Japanese Contemporary Art, Taegu Art & Culture Hall, Taegu, South Korea, 1997

Sigg, Uli, Harald Szeemann, Li Xianting, Yi Ying, Hou Hanru, Alanna Heiss and Ai Weiwei, Chinese Artists: Texts And Interviews, Timezone 8, Beijing, 2004

Sullivan, Michael, Modern Chinese Artists: A Biographical Dictionary, University of California, Berkeley, 2003

Szeemann, Harald, Dapertutto/Aperto overall/ Aperto partout/Aperto uberall, Venice Biennale and Marsilio, 1999

Teerlinck, Hilde, and Qin Jan, Printemps de Chine, CRAC Alsace, Altkirch, France, 2003

Tinari, Philip, and Mario Ciampi, Artists in China, Verba Volant, Florence, 2007

Van Dijk, Hans, Jochen Nothand and Andrea Schmid, China Avantgarde, Edition Braus, Heidelberg, 1993

Wise, Peter, Christopher Makos and Ai Weiwei, Andy Warhol in China, Timezone 8, Beijing, 2008

Wu Hung, Huangsheng, and Feng Boyi, Reinterpretation: A Decade of Experimental Chinese Art (1990-2000), Guangzhou Triennial, 2002

Xie Nanxing, Ai Weiwei and Nataline Colonnello, Xie Nanxing: Paintings 1992-2004, Timezone 8 and Galerie Urs Meile, Beijing, 2006

Zyman, Daniela, and Gabrielle Cram, Shooting Back, Thyssen-Bornemisza Contemporary Art, Vienna, 2007

SELECTED ARTICLES AND REVIEWS

Adam, Georgina, et al., 'The Power 100', Art Review, October 2007

Adam, Hubertus, 'Follies am Flussufer: Jinhua Architectural Park 2004-2006', Archithese, 8 August 2007

Ai Weiwei, 'Production Notes', Artforum, October 2007

Ai Weiwei, 'Influence: Today or Tomorrow', Art Asia Pacific Almanac, no. 3, 2008

Ai Weiwei, Amy Cappellazzo, Thomas Crow, Donna De Salvo, Isabelle Graw, Dakis Joannou, Robert Pincus-Witten, James Meyer and Tim Griffin, 'Art and its Markets: A Roundtable Discussion', Artforum, April 2008

Aloi, Daniel, 'Ai Weiwei: Smashing China's traditions in art and architecture', World Literature Today, July 2007

Altorfer, Sabine, 'Lieber Träume als Gemurmel. Documenta 12 Kassel. Die Weltkunstausstellung verdient die Bezeichnung "global". Die Show der Unbekannten hat aber einen heimlichen Star', Berner Rundschau, 15 June 2007

Ansfield, Jonathan, and Don Hewitt, 'Architects on the Ramparts of the Chinese Design Revolution: Draftsmen's Contract', Newsweek, 13 August 2007

Audédat, Michel, 'L' art c'est aussi du vent', L'Hebdo, 28 June 2007

Baker, R. C., 'Best in Show: Ai Weiwei "Illumination"', Village Voice, 9 April 2008

Bassets, Marc, 'Kassel y el viento creador: El artista chino Ai Weiwei asegura que su escultura "Plantilla" gana en expresividad tras su destrucción accidental', La Vanguardia, 24 June 2007

Birnie Danzker, Jo Anne, 'Documenta 12', Yishu Journal of Contemporary Chinese Art, autumn 2007

Blume, Georg, 'Ich habe einen Traum: Ai Weiwei', Zeitmagazin, 26 July 2007

Bork, Henrik, 'Wir bringen unsere eigenen Köche mit', Tages-Anzeiger, April 2007

Boucher, Brian, 'Ai Weiwei at Mary Boone', Art in America, June 2008

Chang, Patty, 'Ai Weiwei', Contemporary Art & Investment, no. 2, 2007

Coggins, David, 'Ai Weiwei's Humane Conceptualism', Art in America, September 2007

Colonnello, Nataline, 'Beyond the Checkmate', Art Asia Pacific, no. 40, 2004

Colonnello, Nataline, and Huang, S., 'Fragment Conversation between Xiao Ling and Ai Weiwei', Art Today, no. 2, 2006

Colonnello, Nataline, 'Figments of Fragments: Ai Weiwei on his first Chinese mainland solo exhibition', That's Beijing, April 2006

Colonnello, Nataline, 'Ai Weiwei: Kippe', Contemporary Art & Investment, no. 1, 2007

Colonnello, Nataline, 'Ai Weiwei', Contemporary, no. 96, 2008

Cotter, Holland, 'Asking serious questions in a very quiet voice', New York Times, 22 June 2007

De Muynck, Bert, 'I jumped on the wrong train: Ai Weiwei looks back on his short but intense career as an architect', Mark Magazine, no. 12, 2008

Duff, Stacey, 'Capital Comeback: They are two of China's most influential artists but Ai Weiwei and Zhu Wie are yet to have a solo exhibit in their home city', Time Out Beijing, no. 19, 2006

Feng, Boyi, 'Some Remarks on Ai Weiwei', Beijing Art Gallery Magazine, no. 112/13, 2007

Fibicher, Bernard, 'Ai Weiwei', Berner Kunstmitteilungen, no. 342, 2004

Fu, Xiaodong, 'From the Inside of Life: About Documenta 12', Art China, no. 4, 2007

'Galleries – Chelsea: Ai Weiwei', The New Yorker, 7 April 2008

Grima, Joseph, 'Ai Weiwei', Icon, no. 57, March 2008

Nav, Haq, 'Yes again, and this time it's for real: An interview with Simon Groom and Karen Smith', Yishu Journal of Contemporary Chinese Art, summer 2007

Harris, Gareth, 'Ai Weiwei condems Beijing Olympics', The Art Newspaper, 1 September 2007

Hart, Sara, '2008 Beijing Olympics: Innovative Architecture ready to change the Face on an Ancient City', Architectural Record, 2004

Henkes, Alice, 'Ai Weiwei in der Kunsthalle Bern', Kunst Bulletin, May 2004

Herzog, Jacques, 'Concept and Fake', Parkett, no. 82, December 2007

Holmes, Pernilla, 'Cultural Revelation: Collectors are looking east, curators are scoping out the hot new talents, and Saatchi is learning the lingo', Time Out London, 1 October 2007

Hosch, Alexander, 'Ai Weiwei: China's Renaissance Man', Architectural Digest, March 2007

Hu, James, and Julia He, 'A Modern Fairytale Concerning One Thousand and One Men: An Interview with Chinese Contemporary Artist Ai Weiwei', Beijing Art Gallery Magazine, 2007

Jasper, Adam, 'Critical Mass: Ai Weiwei', Art Review, no. 22, May 2008

Jocks, H. N., 'Ai Weiwei: Das Märchen von 1001 Chinesen. Ein Gespräch mit Heinz Nobert Jocks', Kunstforum International, no. 187, August-September 2007

Jun, Jun, 'No Frontiers/No Limits: The Artwork of Ai Weiwei', Artco Magazine, May 2006

Kelley, Jeff, 'Ai Weiwei: Look Back', Artforum, September 2008

Krueger, J., 'Ai Weiwei', Perspective, October 2006

Krueger, J., 'Soul Reversal', Perspective, October 2006

Kunz, S., 'Aufbruch in China', Art, no. 5, 2000

Lau, P., 'Ein Besuch der Documenta 12, unter Berücksichtigung von Ai Weiwei', Kassels Schlagzeilenproduzent, no. 1, 2007

Leanza, Beatrice, 'Ai Weiwei at Galerie Urs Meile, Beijing', Flash Art, no. 249, July-September 2006

Lewis, A., 'China Now', South China Morning Post, 3 March 2003

Lorch, Catrin, 'Formvollendeter Allgemeinzustand der Welt: die Documenta', Kunst Bulletin, July-August 2007

Lu, Carol, 'The inflated business of China contemporary art', Contemporary, no. 80, 2006

Lu, Carol, 'Mr. Big', Frieze, June-August 2008

Lu, Heng-Zhong, 'An Interview with Ai Weiwei, one of the architects of Jinhua Architecture Park, Zhejiang', Time + Architecture, no. 1, 2006

Maak, Niklas, 'Das Geschenk der Wettergötter. Produktives Scheitern ist ein Grundmotiv dieser Documenta. Bei Ai Weiwei's Skulptur hat nun ein Unwetter nachgebessert', Frankfurter Allgemeine Zeitung, 22 June 2007

Maak, Niklas, 'Die Documenta 2007 ruft zum grossen Marsch', Frankfurter Allgemeine Zeitung, no. 70, 2007

Maerkle, Andrew, 'In Search of the Real Thing', Art Asia Pacific, no. 53, 2007

Manonelles Moner, Laia, 'Cómo se rompe un jarrón chino?', Art & Co, no. 3, 2008

Melvin, Sheila, 'Framing Photos as Art in China', Herald International Tribune, 8 August 2007

Merewether, Charles, 'Ai Weiwei: The Freedom of Irreverence', Art Asia Pacific, no. 53, 2007

Merewether, Charles, 'Made in China', Parkett, no. 82, December 2007

Mingels, Guido, 'Ein Nest für das neue China', Das Magazin, 2007

Mingels, Guido, 'Pekings Olympiastadion: Vorzeigearchitektur für eine Diktatur und die Frage an deren Schweizer Schöpfer. Darf man das bauen? Vogelnest und Kuckucksei', Der Tagesspiegel, 8 August 2007

Münter, Ulrike, 'Märchen mal anders', Die Tageszeitung, 11 June 2007

Münter, Ulrike, 'Die Kunst der Beschleunigung', Berliner Zeitung, 3 May 2006

Neidhart, Christoph, 'Der Chinesentransporter', Weltwoche, 22 July 2007

Obrist, Hans Ulrich, 'Ai Weiwei', Domus, no. 894, July-August 2006

Pasternack, Alex, 'Reluctant Return for a Beijing Provocateur', New York Sun, 7 March 2008

Péus, Camilla, 'Kunstkaiser', Architektur und Wohnen, no. 3, 2007

Politi, Giancarlo, and Andrea Bellini, 'Planet China', Flash Art, no. 252, January-February 2007

Pollack, Barbara, 'A Bowl of Pearls, a Ton of Tea, and an Olympic Stadium', Artnews, October 2006

Pollack, Barbara, 'Art's New Superpower', Vanity Fair, December 2007

Pollack, Barbara, 'Ai Weiwei Illumination', Time Out New York, 10 April 2008

Robecchi, Michele, 'Chinese Art at the End of the Millennium', Flash Art, no. 217, March-April 2001

Ruf, Beatrix, 'Kunst ist, was man Kunst nennt: Nürnberger Nachrichten', Magazin am Wochenende, no. 231, 2007

Schindhelm, Michael, 'Der gehäutete Volkskörper', Basler Zeitung Kulturmagazin, 16 October 2004

Schreiber, Anne, 'Keine Kunst ohne Risiko. Warum Starkünster Ai Weiwei 1001 Chinesen zur Documenta nach Kassel holt und was das mit Kultur zu tun hat: ein Experiment mit ungewissem Ausgang', Handelsblatt, 14 June 2007

Siemon, Mark, 'Wir werden viel Spass haben', Frankfurter Allgemeine Sonntagszeitung, no. 12, 2007

Siemon, Mark, 'Olympische neue Weltordnung', Frankfurter Allgemeine Zeitung, no. 236, 2007

Siemon, Mark, 'Olympisches Lexikon', Frankfurter Allgemeine Zeitung, 1 April 2008

Simon, Sean, 'Ai Weiwei's heart belongs to Dada', Artspeak, 16 March 1988

Smith, Karen, 'Ai Weiwei Solo Exhibition at Urs Meile Galerie', Time Out Beijing, no. 19, 2007

Smith, Karen, 'Where Architects Fear to Tred', Art India, April 2008

Smith, Karen, 'Ai Weiwei: 21st Century Beijing Man', Artist Profile, no. 3, April 2008

Spalding, David, 'Dream Factory, Rubbish Heap', Contemporary, no. 72, 2005

Spalding, David, 'Ai Weiwei', Artforum, September 2006

Spalding, David, 'Guan Yi', Contemporary, no. 80, 2006

Spinelli, Claudia, 'Mao am Ende: Chinas Künstler beruhigen den Besserwestler mit Sozialistenpop. Einer aber erweist sich am Schlitzohr: Ai Weiwei', Die Weltwoche, 2004

Tinari, Philip, 'China Power and Chinese Power', Fused Magazine, 2006

Tinari, Philip, 'Made in China: The status symbol in the West is a work of art from the East', New York Times, 25 February 2007

Tinari, Philip, 'A Kind of True Living', Artforum, summer 2007

Tinari, Philip, 'Some Simple Reflections on an Artist in a City 2001-2007', Parkett, no. 82, December 2007

Tobler, Konrad, 'Manche hatten nicht einmal einen Namen: Der Luzerner Galerist Urs Meile über die 1001 Chinesen, die für die Documenta nach Kassel reisen', Berne Sonntags Zeitung, 27 May 2007

Toy, Mary-Anne, 'The Artist as an Angry Man', The Age, 19 January 2008

Tung, D., 'It's all about Destiny! Isn't It?', ArtChina, no. 4, 2007

Vine, Richard, 'The Way We Were, The Way We Are', Art in America, June 2008

Von Taube, Annika, 'Happily ever after? Will the Documenta change 1001 Chinese lives?', Sleek Magazine, no. 2, 2007

Watts, Jonathan, 'Olympic Artist attacks China's Pomp and Propaganda: Man behind Bird's Nest Stadium to boycott Games', The Guardian, 9 August 2007

Welti, Alfred, 'Der Kaiser von Kassel', Art, no. 8, 2007

Widmann, Arno, 'Es lebe der Sturm: Der chinesische Künstler Ai Weiwei lobt den Kasseler Wettergott, der sein Documenta-Werk fällte', Frankfurter Rundschau, no. 142, 2007

Wu, Penghui, 'I am an ant not bound to any group', Hiart Magazine Beijing, no. 13, 2007

Yao, Pauline Jiashan, 'Between Truth and Fiction: Notes on Fakes, Copies, and Authenticity in Contemporary Chinese Art', Yishu: Journal of Contemporary Chinese Art, summer 2005

Yao, Pauline Jiashan, 'Ai Weiwei', Contemporary Art & Investment, April 2007

Zanoni, F., 'La retromarcia di Ai Weiwei', Il Sole 24 Ore, 25 September 2007

MUSEUM FÜR MODERNE KUNST, Frankfurt am Main

MUSEUM OF CONTEMPORARY ART, Los Angeles

SOLOMON R. GUGGENHEIM MUSEUM, New York

TATE, London

ULLENS CENTER FOR CONTEMPORARY ART, Beijing

PHAIDON PRESS LTD.
REGENT'S WHARF
ALL SAINTS STREET
LONDON N1 9PA

PHAIDON PRESS INC.
180 VARICK STREET
NEW YORK, NY 10014

WWW.PHAIDON.COM

First published 2009
© 2009 Phaidon Press Limited
All works of Ai Weiwei are ©
Ai Weiwei

ISBN:
978-0-7148-4889-1

A CIP catalogue record of
this book is available from the
British Library.

Designed by Emma Chiu and
Melanie Mues, Mues Design,
London

Printed in Hong Kong

PUBLISHER'S
ACKNOWLEDGEMENTS

Special thanks to Carol Lu;
Urs Meile and Karin Seiz at
Urs Meile Gallery; Gao Yuan,
Nadine Stenke and Zhao Zhao
of FAKE Team; Philip Tinari.

We would also like to thank
the following for lending
reproductions:
Paul Green, Nick Haymes,
Nicolas Lackner, Kevin Langan,
Adam Reich, Greg Weight.

ARTIST'S
ACKNOWLEDGEMENTS

Ai Weiwei would like to thank
Craig Garrett and Michele
Robecchi at Phaidon Press.

All works are in private
collections unless otherwise
stated.

CONTEMPORARY ARTISTS:

Contemporary Artists is a series of authoritative and extensively illustrated studies of today's most important artists. Each title offers a comprehensive survey of an individual artist's work and a range of art writing contributed by an international spectrum of authors, all leading figures in their fields, from art history and criticism to philosophy, cultural theory and fiction. Each study provides incisive analysis and multiple perspectives on contemporary art and its inspiration. These are essential source books for everyone concerned with art today.

MARINA ABRAMOVIĆ KRISTINE STILES, KLAUS BIESENBACH, CHRISSIE ILES / VITO ACCONCI FRAZER WARD, MARK C. TAYLOR, JENNIFER BLOOMER / AI WEIWEI KAREN SMITH, HANS ULRICH OBRIST, BERNARD FIBICHER / DOUG AITKEN DANIEL BIRNBAUM, AMANDA SHARP, JÖRG HEISER / FRANCIS ALŸS RUSSELL FERGUSON, CUAUHTÉMOC MEDINA, JEAN FISHER / UTA BARTH PAMELA M. LEE, MATTHEW HIGGS, JEREMY GILBERT-ROLFE / CHRISTIAN BOLTANSKI DIDIER SEMIN, TAMAR GARB, DONALD KUSPIT / LOUISE BOURGEOIS ROBERT STORR, PAULO HERKENHOFF (WITH THYRZA GOODEVE), ALLAN SCHWARTZMAN / CAI GUO-QIANG DANA FRIIS-HANSEN, OCTAVIO ZAYA, TAKASHI SERIZAWA / MAURIZIO CATTELAN FRANCESCO BONAMI, NANCY SPECTOR, BARBARA VANDERLINDEN, MASSIMILIANO GIONI VIJA CELMINS LANE RELYEA, ROBERT GOBER, BRIONY FER / RICHARD DEACON JON THOMPSON, PIER LUIGI TAZZI, PETER SCHJELDAHL, PENELOPE CURTIS TACITA DEAN JEAN-CHRISTOPHE ROYOUX, MARINA WARNER, GERMAINE GREER / MARK DION LISA GRAZIOSE CORRIN, MIWON KWON, NORMAN BRYSON / PETER DOIG ADRIAN SEARLE, KITTY SCOTT, CATHERINE GRENIER / STAN DOUGLAS SCOTT WATSON, DIANA THATER, CAROL J. CLOVER / MARLENE DUMAS DOMINIC VAN DEN BOOGERD, BARBARA BLOOM, MARIUCCIA CASADIO, ILARIA BONACOSSA / JIMMIE DURHAM LAURA MULVEY, DIRK SNAUWAERT, MARK ALICE DURANT / OLAFUR ELIASSON MADELEINE GRYNSZTEJN, DANIEL BIRNBAUM, MICHAEL SPEAKS / PETER FISCHLI AND DAVID WEISS ROBERT FLECK, BEATE SÖNTGEN, ARTHUR C. DANTO / TOM FRIEDMAN BRUCE HAINLEY, DENNIS COOPER, ADRIAN SEARLE / ISA GENZKEN ALEX FARQUHARSON, DIEDRICH DIEDERICHSEN, SABINE BREITWIESER ANTONY GORMLEY JOHN HUTCHINSON, SIR ERNST GOMBRICH, LELA B. NJATIN, W. J. T. MITCHELL / DAN GRAHAM BIRGIT PELZER, MARK FRANCIS, BEATRIZ COLOMINA / PAUL GRAHAM ANDREW WILSON, GILLIAN WEARING, CAROL SQUIERS / HANS HAACKE WALTER GRASSKAMP, MOLLY NESBIT, JON BIRD / MONA HATOUM GUY BRETT, MICHAEL ARCHER, CATHERINE DE ZEGHER / THOMAS HIRSCHHORN BENJAMIN H. D. BUCHLOH, ALISON M. GINGERAS, CARLOS BASUALDO JENNY HOLZER DAVID JOSELIT, JOAN SIMON, RENATA SALECL / RONI HORN LOUISE NERI, LYNNE COOKE, THIERRY DE DUVE / ILYA KABAKOV BORIS GROYS, DAVID A. ROSS, IWONA BLAZWICK / ALEX KATZ CARTER RATCLIFF, ROBERT STORR, IWONA BLAZWICK / ON KAWARA JONATHAN WATKINS, 'TRIBUTE', RENÉ DENIZOT / MIKE KELLEY JOHN C. WELCHMAN, ISABELLE GRAW, ANTHONY VIDLER / MARY KELLY MARGARET IVERSEN, DOUGLAS CRIMP, HOMI K. BHABHA / WILLIAM KENTRIDGE DAN CAMERON, CAROLYN CHRISTOV-BAKARGIEV, J. M. COETZEE / YAYOI KUSAMA LAURA HOPTMAN, AKIRA TATEHATA, UDO KULTERMANN / CHRISTIAN MARCLAY JENNIFER GONZALEZ, KIM GORDON, MATTHEW HIGGS / PAUL MCCARTHY RALPH RUGOFF, KRISTINE STILES, GIACINTO DI PIETRANTONIO / CILDO MEIRELES PAULO HERKENHOFF, GERARDO MOSQUERA, DAN CAMERON / LUCY ORTA ROBERTO PINTO, NICOLAS BOURRIAUD, MAIA DAMIANOVIC / JORGE PARDO CHRISTINE VÉGH, LANE RELYEA, CHRIS KRAUS / RAYMOND PETTIBON ROBERT STORR, DENNIS COOPER, ULRICH LOOCK / RICHARD PRINCE ROSETTA BROOKS, JEFF RIAN, LUC SANTE / PIPILOTTI RIST PEGGY PHELAN, HANS ULRICH OBRIST, ELIZABETH BRONFEN / ANRI SALA MARK GODFREY, HANS ULRICH OBRIST, LIAM GILLICK / DORIS SALCEDO NANCY PRINCENTHAL, CARLOS BASUALDO, ANDREAS HUYSSEN / THOMAS SCHÜTTE JULIAN HEYNEN, JAMES LINGWOOD, ANGELA VETTESE / STEPHEN SHORE MICHAEL FRIED, CHRISTY LANGE, JOEL STERNFELD / ROMAN SIGNER GERHARD MACK, PAULA VAN DEN BOSCH, JEREMY MILLAR / LORNA SIMPSON KELLIE JONES, THELMA GOLDEN, CHRISSIE ILES / NANCY SPERO JON BIRD, JO ANNA ISAAK, SYLVÈRE LOTRINGER / JESSICA STOCKHOLDER BARRY SCHWABSKY, LYNNE TILLMAN, LYNNE COOKE / WOLFGANG TILLMANS JAN VERWOERT, PETER HALLEY, MIDORI MATSUI / LUC TUYMANS ULRICH LOOCK, JUAN VICENTE ALIAGA, NANCY SPECTOR, HANS RUDOLF REUST / JEFF WALL THIERRY DE DUVE, ARIELLE PELENC, BORIS GROYS, JEAN-FRANÇOIS CHEVRIER / GILLIAN WEARING RUSSELL FERGUSON, DONNA DE SALVO, JOHN SLYCE / LAWRENCE WEINER ALEXANDER ALBERRO AND ALICE ZIMMERMAN, BENJAMIN H. D. BUCHLOH, DAVID BATCHELOR FRANZ WEST ROBERT FLECK, BICE CURIGER, NEAL BENEZRA